Teaching
Mathematics
with
Manipulatives

Teaching

MATHEMATICS

with

MANIPULATIVES

A Resource of Activities for the K–12 Teacher

MARK A. SPIKELL

George Mason University

Allyn and Bacon

Boston London Toronto Sydney Tokyo Singapore

Copyright © 1993 by Allyn and Bacon
A Division of Simon & Schuster, Inc.
160 Gould Street
Needham Heights, Massachusetts 02194

Library of Congress Cataloging-in-Publication Data

Spikell, Mark A.
    Teaching mathematics with manipulatives : a resource of activities for the K–12 teacher / Mark A. Spikell.
        p. cm.
    ISBN 0-205-13993-0
    1. Mathematics—Study and teaching—Audio-visual aids. I. Title.
QA18.S65 1993
510′.71′2—dc20   92-19589
                                                                  CIP

Printed in the United States of America

10 9 8 7 6 5 4 3 2   96 95 94

Photographs on pages 16 and 57 (Figures 2.4, 3.1, 3.2, and 3.3) are by Jim Scourletis. Materials for photography provided by Cuisenaire Company of America, Inc., White Plains, New York.

C O N T E N T S

Preface   vii

CHAPTER ONE   Introduction: How to Use This Book   1

CHAPTER TWO   Motivating the Pythagorean Theorem
               with Geoboards   11

    Section A   The Problem   13
    Section B   Unit Objectives   13
    Section C   Materials Required   14
    Section D   Description of Geoboards   16
    Section E   The Sequence of Activities   17
    Section F   Extensions   51

CHAPTER THREE   Motivating Pascal's Triangle   53

    Section A   The Problem   55
    Section B   Unit Objectives   55
    Section C   The Materials   56
    Section D   Description of the Cubes   56
    Section E   The Sequence of Activities   58
    Section F   Extensions   88

CHAPTER FOUR   Discovering an Application for the
                Formula $Y = 2^{(n-1)}$ with Cuisenaire Rods   101

    Section A   The Problem   103
    Section B   Unit Objectives   103
    Section C   Materials Required   104
    Section D   Description of Cuisenaire Rods   104

Section E   The Sequence of Activities   107
Section F   Extensions   148

CHAPTER FIVE   Exploring Combinations with Attribute Blocks   153

Section A   The Problem   155
Section B   Unit Objectives   155
Section C   Materials Required   156
Section D   Description of Attribute Blocks   156
Section E   The Sequence of Activities   161
Section F   Extensions   208

CHAPTER SIX   Prologue: Why the Frame-of-Reference
Model?   213

P R E F A C E

Several years ago, at the annual meeting of the National Council Teachers of Mathematics, I had lunch with a long-time friend and professional colleague, Dr. Linda Schulman, a professor at Lesley College in Cambridge, Massachusetts. In the course of our conversation I asked Linda what she thought of my new writing project, the effort to prepare this text. Though I do not recall her specific words, I remember vividly the gist of her response.

"Mark," she asked, "are you sure you can devote the amount of time it will take for you to prepare the type of in-depth materials for teachers you are planning?"

My response was an emphatic, immediate, "Yes, of course!" I was certain the project would not take nearly as long as Linda's question implied. As I sit here thinking about it today, the tone of my response surely must have conveyed the message, "Why in the world would you even ask such a question?"

Well, Linda, here for the first time, and publicly, let me say that I know why you asked the question, and if my answer was too abrupt, I apologize. Little did I know then how wise and on target your question and your message were.

This project has truly been a labor of love, the demands of which I never could have anticipated. The manuscript went through several drafts in preparation, numerous reviews, field testing with teachers, numerous rewrites, figure preparation, and all the other myriad tasks required to place a text in print these days.

As if all these expected tasks were not enough, Murphy's law played a role as well. At just the moment I was ready to prepare and print final drafts, offices at the university were moved, some computer equipment previously accessible was no longer available, and new computer equipment required different software. Have you ever had to change software, even just make an update, in the middle of a huge project? Well, don't.

Of course, now that the authoring is over, I have no real complaints. Those who write regularly should know that authoring isn't nearly as easy and painless as it seems to the reader (Dr.

Schulman's point, perhaps). But during the writing process there were times, indeed, when I thought of abandoning the project. And I admit freely that I woefully underestimated the time it would take to put my new frame-of-reference model ideas into publishable form. Maybe that is one reason that so few materials are prepared in such depth. To do so well does require a great deal of time.

Still, I am truly happy that I persevered. The type of materials represented by the frame-of-reference model on which this book is based are desperately needed by educators at all levels who desire to teach mathematics effectively using manipulatives. The frame-of-reference model is explained in Chapter 6, the Prologue to this book, and each of the units in Chapters 2–5 is based on the model. I hope that other authors will agree that in-depth materials are valuable and that many more books of this type will be written by colleagues in the profession.

It is traditional to close a preface by thanking those who helped in the effort. That is a tradition I am truly pleased to follow. I only hope that I have not overlooked acknowledging anyone who contributed to the success of this endeavor.

First and foremost, it is my family who deserve the credit for this book reaching the publication stage. Linda Schulman's point about the time the project would take most affected my wife, Laurie, and my children, Eli and Emily. Like most university- and school-based authors, I had to write this book in addition to, not as a replacement for, my normal duties as a university professor—teaching, research, and service. Thus, my writing time had to come primarily from family time. Countless evenings, weekends, holidays, and other family time occasions over several years were devoted to the book rather than to the family. For their patience and acceptance, if not their understanding, of an undesirable circumstance, I will be forever grateful.

I am also indebted to several university colleagues, both teachers and former students, who were willing to read various versions of the manuscript and provide suggestions, many of which were incorporated into the text. It would be impossible to mention all of them, but the contributions of the following were particularly helpful. I thank them for their time and interest in the text. Without their valuable practitioners' insight, the material would hardly be as refined as it is.

1. Marilyn Sheller, Special Projects Mathematics Teacher, Fairfax County Public School System

2. Renee F. Herndon, sixth-grade teacher, Holmes Middle School, Fairfax County Public School System
3. Patricia Ann Wright, Gifted and Talented Itinerant Teacher, grades 4 through 6, Newington Forest Elementary School, Fairfax County Public School System
4. Juneanne Demek, fifth-grade teacher, London Towne Elementary School, Fairfax County Public School System
5. Laura M. Clairmont, Learning Disabilities Resource Teacher, Sunrise Valley Elementary School, Fairfax County Public School System
6. Christine Fernsler, grade 1 teacher and math coordinator K–4, Sidwell Friends School, Washington, D.C.
7. Dr. Klaus Fischer, associate professor of mathemathics, George Mason University, Fairfax, Virginia
8. Dr. Randall I. Charles, professor, San Jose State University, San Jose, California

A special note of thanks goes to Jennifer Voss, an undergraduate student in my course, "Teaching Problem Solving in School Mathematics." In addition to her excellent work with manipulatives in my course, Jennifer was wonderfully computer-literate and could handle sophisticated graphics programs with ease. She is responsible for the excellent figures (would you believe, Jennifer, 150 of them?) in the text.

To Mary Blackwell, office support coordinator in the George Mason University Computer Support Services Division, and to all of the staff (particularly Kathy Gillette and May Thompson) who helped type early versions of the manuscript and returned them to me on floppy disks for my machine, you saved me many hours of effort. Thanks—it was appreciated.

Acknowledgments for valuable assistance must include a note of appreciation to Dr. Albert Edgemon, then chairman of the Department of Curriculum and Instruction at George Mason University; to Sue Woodfine, departmental lead secretary; and to all my colleagues in the Graduate School of Education. The access Dr. Edgemon provided to needed computing equipment at absolutely critical times was invaluable. And Sue, her numerous able staff associates and my many faculty colleagues were generous beyond the norm in accommodating my presence in "their space" using "their equipment" for so many months.

Of course, no expression of thanks for support should fail to include the efforts of one's publisher. In this case it is a real pleasure to single out the efforts of Mylan Jaixen and his able assistants, Deborah Reinke and Susan Hutchinson. Mylan's support of this project from acquisition through publication has been wonderful, and Deborah's early assistance and Susan's follow-up were top-notch in every respect. Additionally, without the excellent work and assistance of Judy Ashkenaz of Total Concept Associates, who handled the editorial production, this book would never have been completed. Thanks to all of you for helping to make my frame-of-reference vision a reality.

In closing, I offer my special thanks to the management and staff of the Laurel Sports Palace, my office away from the office, where the ambiance, service, food, and opportunity to "watch some sports too," made writing the initial drafts on the weekends possible and modestly pleasant.

Mark A. Spikell
George Mason University
Fairfax, Virginia

Teaching Mathematics with Manipulatives

CHAPTER ONE

INTRODUCTION
How to Use
This Book

The collection of lessons in this book offers one method for teachers and prospective teachers to obtain significant insight into the information they need to use manipulatives effectively in a classroom. The book is a resource for helping teachers at any level to see how manipulatives can be and have been used in classroom settings to teach specific mathematical and problem-solving topics.

Each chapter presents a lesson just as it might be used in a classroom setting to teach a mathematics topic using manipulatives. Each of the lessons is presented for teachers as a *frame-of-reference model* (see the Prologue, Chapter 6, for a discussion of the model). The lessons are presented in sufficient detail to enable teachers to modify or even replicate them for use in their own classroom settings. Many teachers will be able to teach the units as they are presented in this book with little modification. For many others, the units are far more valuable as idea generators or frames of reference that provide insight into how to think about developing one's own manipulative-based classroom units.

Each unit provides a comprehensive, thorough treatment of the way in which a particular manipulative can be incorporated into teaching mathematics in a classroom. Further, each unit presents specific mathematics content and a precise description of a sequence of activities for teaching the content using a manipulative. Importantly, the activities in this resource book have actually been presented to teachers, prospective teachers, or school-aged students. Also included with each unit are the actual responses one might expect based on the answers given by the learners with whom the activities were tested.

Because of the important role of problem solving in the modern school mathematics program, the sequence of activities presented in each lesson has been designed to engage students actively in problem solving. In fact, each lesson has as a primary objective the goal of familiarizing students with such important problem-solving methods as collecting data, organizing data, making tables, analyzing data, looking for patterns, forming conjectures, making and verifying hypotheses, and stating conclusions. Thus, in addition to providing examples of discovery lessons that help teach mathematics content with manipulatives, the lessons in this text provide classroom-tested activities for teaching problem-solving ideas and strategies to students.

One good way to use this text to improve the teaching of mathematics and problem solving with manipulatives is to follow these steps:

1. Glance over or read the chapter (model lessons) quickly to obtain an overall sense of the unit development.

2. Return to the unit and consider more carefully the sequence of activities in the development. At this stage, it will be evident which portions of the development the reader needs to read carefully and which portions may be skimmed or even skipped altogether.

3. Work through each activity by actually using the mathematics manipulative.

4. Refer as needed to the various tables and figures provided. Extensive figures and tables are given for the benefit of those who will find them useful in understanding the presentation. Often they provide an excellent means of self-checking ones own work effort in attempting to solve or explore the problem under consideration.

5. Experiment with offering the unit (or appropriate parts) to students. In doing so, freely modify the exploration as necessary for the age and mathematics background of students in your particular classroom. Each of the units, or significant parts of each unit, can be adapted for use in early childhood, middle, junior high, or high school grades. Moreover, all of the lessons are suitable for use in teacher education classes or inservice staff development workshops for elementary or secondary school teachers.

It is important for readers to note that the model lessons in this book are purposely written in thorough, comprehensive detail. This enables teachers with varying levels of knowledge about mathematics and a range of differing experiences using manipulatives to utilize this resource book. Some teachers with strong mathematics backgrounds and considerable experience with manipulatives may not require the step-by-step development. These teachers are encouraged to skim or even skip selected portions of each chapter as appropriate. Other teachers will find it helpful to read all the parts of each model lesson in order to understand the mathematics presented and how to use the manipulative to teach that mathematics.

Key Assumptions on Which This Book Is Based

In writing this book, I have been guided by several key ideas about what constitutes good teaching and learning in school mathematics. These ideas include the following:

1. **Model effective teaching.**

    If we have ideas about what and how teachers should teach school mathematics to students, then we should teach teachers the same information in the same ways. By so educating teachers, we teach them the mathematics content they need and provide models of good teaching which they may be able to replicate or adapt in their own settings. The units in this text, though designed for adult learners, are presented as they could be presented to students of various ages. Readers can, if they wish, use the ideas discussed here just as they are presented in their own classrooms.

2. **Promote active versus passive learning.**

    The ancient Chinese proverb

    > I hear and I forget;
    > I see and I remember;
    > I do and I understand.

    is frequently cited to make the point that children learn best when they are active rather than passive learners. I am convinced that the same is true for adults. If we want them to master the content associated with manipulatives and effective ways of using manipulatives to teach school mathematics, then we must actively engage adults in the learning process. We do so not by lecturing or telling but, rather, by employing a range of instructional techniques, including workshops, laboratory explorations, small-group activities, and cooperative learning projects, that force them to participate actively in learning. The units in this text are designed to engage the adult or student learner in open-ended problem-solving activities requiring hands-on explorations with manipulatives.

3. **Utilize discovery methods.**

    For large-group instruction, guided discovery provides an excellent method for teaching with manipulatives. Briefly, guided discovery learning involves establishing instructional objectives, designing a sequence of activities to reach those objectives, leading students through the activities using questioning rather than "telling" techniques, and helping students to formulate and state their own conclusions or answers to the questions. When this sequence of steps is done properly, students have an opportunity to learn actively by doing and thinking rather than passively by listening, even in large-group instructional settings. Hence, the units in this text are designed using the discovery method as the primary instructional technique.

4. **Provide concrete to abstract experiences.**

Most learners, whether adults or children, will master mathematical concepts and skills more readily if they are presented (or reviewed) first in concrete, pictorial, and symbolic forms. By using manipulatives, pictures, and symbols to model or represent abstract ideas, we set the stage for learners to understand the abstractions they represent. Thus, activities designed for learning mathematics should include appropriate phases involving the manipulation of concrete objects, the drawing of pictures, and the writing of words and numbers before abstract concepts are discussed or taught. The units in this book rely heavily on the reader manipulating objects and viewing figures in the learning process. In that regard, the text contains complete drawings and figures for most of the problems and solutions that are discussed.

5. **Focus on problem solving.**

The study of mathematics should focus on problem solving in much the same way as the study of science should focus on laboratory experimentation. Students should be given problems to solve that require meaningful exploration, data collection, data recording, analysis, hypothesis formation, proof, and the reporting of conclusions. Students should be encouraged to engage actively in the process of solving such problems through individual and small-group work, and they should be given opportunities to discuss their efforts orally. Finally, students should be encouraged to develop the ability to communicate in writing both the results of their effort and the procedures used in solving the problem, much as science students are expected to write lab reports. Hence, the units in this text are designed to enable teachers to teach problem solving as well as the mathematics associated with the activities.

6. **Provide sample lessons and units.**

Using manipulatives in teaching is as much an art as a science. It takes a great deal of knowledge, insight, and skill to incorporate manipulatives effectively into an instructional program. There are no fixed procedures that can be memorized and invoked to help teachers use manipulatives effectively, and there are few, if any, units or lessons already developed that can be used universally. Nonetheless, we cannot expect teachers to become expert at using manipulatives by osmosis. We must give them sufficiently comprehensive and thorough experiences with manipulatives to enable them to make sound curricular judgments about why, how, and when to use manipulatives. And we must help them learn how to develop their own curriculum materials, units, and lessons. One way to do this is to expose teachers to fully developed units, not to provide material to be copied but to give them starting points that they can modify, adapt, and develop into their own lessons. Hence, the units in this book present a thorough, in-depth presentation so that teachers can view the complete picture and decide for themselves what to eliminate, modify, or include.

7. **Encourage the teaching of topics, not grade levels.**

Most teachers seek information on topics and methods that are specifically applicable to the grades or course they teach. Early childhood teachers want content, activities, and methods they can use with grade K–2 students and junior high school teachers want content, activities, and methods they can use with students in grades 7 and 8. Although manipulatives can effectively be used to teach or review mathematics content at all levels from K to 12, developing units to do so that are grade-level specific is a very complicated and not particularly useful task. What is appropriate in a particular classroom depends on a range of variables, including students' needs, their level of mathematics sophistication, the objectives of the school system, and parents' desires.

Consequently, developing grade-level or course units must ultimately be left to the individual teachers, who know their own students' needs and their local community's objectives. But to be prepared to tailor-make such units, teachers need a comprehensive overview of the range of content topics, activities, and methods that can be associated with a particular manipulative. They should, therefore, be exposed to units that provide thorough comprehensive presentations incorporating content, activities, and methods. Seeing this range gives teachers a complete, in-depth overview, which allows them readily to adapt, modify, and extend what they have learned into appropriate units for students. Hence, the units in this book have been written to cover topics without regard to specific grade levels so that teachers can adapt them for their own classes. Each of the lessons contains significant amounts of material that can be presented in early childhood, the intermediate grades, junior high, high school, or teacher education classes.

Organization of the Book

Each chapter in this book presents a complete unit that has been classroom tested with teachers, prospective teachers, or school-aged students. Each unit includes a thorough exploration and discussion of a problem and its solution using one of four manipulatives—geoboards, Attribute Blocks, Cuisenaire rods, and Color Cubes.

Each exploration and discussion is presented in six sections, as follows:

Section A: The Problem

In this section, a nonroutine problem is presented for solution. The problem can be solved directly using geoboards, Attribute Blocks, Cuisenaire rods, or Color Cubes, or it can be solved using ideas developed with the various manipulatives.

Section B: Unit Objectives

In this section, two types of objectives for the unit are identified—primary objectives and secondary objectives.

Primary objectives are the key mathematical ideas, concepts, principles, or skills that are introduced or reviewed by the problem, problem solution, and presentation given. Primary objectives also include instructional objectives or noncontent goals associated with the exploration in the unit. These goals cover a range of valuable educational benefits, such as focusing on communicating mathematics through writing, providing peer group learning experiences, developing problem-solving abilities, and the like.

Secondary objectives include both content and instructional goals that could be fully developed at the teacher's discretion but have not been developed in the presentation given.

Section C: Materials Required

In this section, the manipulative and all the materials needed for each student to explore the unit are listed. If the unit is presented for either large or small groups, this is indicated, and the amount of materials needed for each group is specified.

Section D: Description of Manipulative

In this section, the manipulative used in the exploration is fully described for the benefit of teachers who may not be familiar with it.

Section E: Sequence of Activities

In this section each unit is fully developed in the form of a sequence of classroom activities as they were actually presented to preservice or inservice teachers or students. The focus is on the actual presentation as it was done (or could be done) with students. A description is given detailing how the activities were introduced, the type of responses to expect, how to guide and motivate students in certain directions, techniques for summarizing the experience, and other relevant observations.

Although the intent here is not to provide a script for others to follow or copy, sufficient information is provided regarding the teaching of the activities to enable most teachers to replicate the units as is or to modify them slightly for their own classrooms.

Also included in this section are observations, comments, and suggestions that may elaborate or extend the ideas presented. These comments are indented and printed in italic type to distinguish them from the text. This will enable readers to know as they read the text which portions are central to the development and which are supplementary.

The observations given are based on the actual experience of having presented the units to teachers or students. Here, the focus is not on how to present the activity but, instead, on the benefits associated with the activities, insights gained from working with students, tips for enhancing student learning, issues generated, and the like.

Section F: **Extensions**

In this section, appropriate follow-on extension problems are given. Generally, these problems review, reinforce, and extend ideas learned by students in the original explorations. Often the extensions enable teachers to present new topics or advanced information as a natural outgrowth of the unit explored. Although extensions are not discussed fully, sufficient information is provided to enable teachers to develop units to explore the ideas suggested.

M O T I V A T I N G
the Pythagorean
Theorem
with Geoboards

CHAPTER CONTENTS

Section A   The Problem

Section B   Unit Objectives

Primary Objectives for This Exploration

Secondary Objectives for This Exploration

Section C   Materials Required

Section D   Description of Geoboards

Section E   Sequence of Activities

Identifying Triangles
Defining Noncongruent Triangles
Counting Right Triangles
Building Squares
Generating Data
Collecting Data
Looking for Patterns
Generalizing the Result and Stating the Conclusion
Solving the Problem

Section F   Extensions

Finding Irrational Lengths
Extending the Pythagorean Relationship
Finding All Noncongruent Right Triangles on a Geoboard

Section A   The Problem

In the triangle in Figure 2.1, what is the length of the third side?

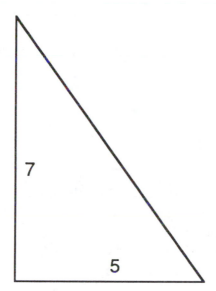

Figure 2.1

Section B   Unit Objectives

Primary Objectives for This Exploration

1. Experiencing the problem-solving steps: (1) understanding a problem, (2) devising a solution plan, (3) experimenting to collect data, (4) organizing the data using pictures and tables, (5) analyzing the data by looking for patterns, (6) forming a hypothesis, and, (7) stating a conclusion.

2. Learning to define geometric figures (right, acute, and obtuse triangles) by looking for similarities and differences in the attributes of each figure.

3. Developing the meaning of the word *different* in the question, "How many different right triangles can you make on a geoboard?"

4. Developing the statement of the Pythagorean theorem in a sequence of activities using geoboards and dot paper.

Secondary Objectives for This Exploration

1. Defining translations, rotations, and reflections.

2. Finding areas of triangles, squares, and rectangles on a geoboard.

3. Introducing irrational numbers to measure the lengths of various segments.

Section C   Materials Needed

5 or more geoboards and rubber bands for the teacher

1 geoboard for each student

6–8 rubber bands for each student

A place card with the words "The A Group" written on it

A place card with the words "The Not A Group" written on it

2 sheets of 5 × 5 geoboard grids for each student or small group (see Figure 2.2)

1 sheet with 10 × 10 dot grids for each student or small group (see Figure 2.3)

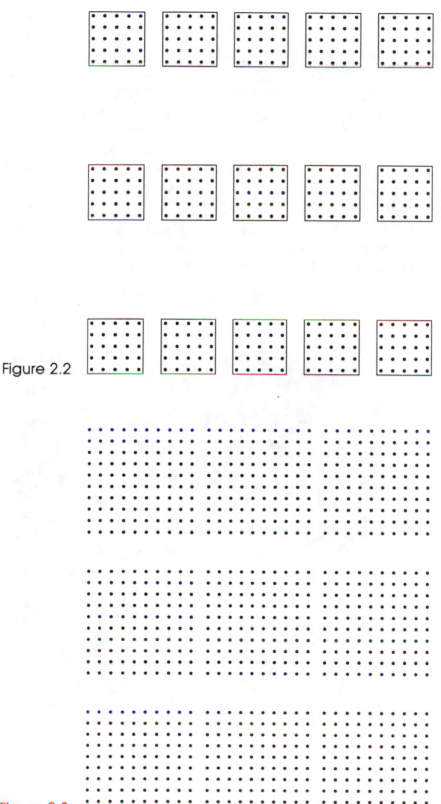

Figure 2.2

Figure 2.3

Section D   Description of Geoboards

Geoboards are plastic or wood boards with square arrangements of pegs or nails. The most common geoboards have pegs or nails that are equally spaced both horizontally and vertically on the board. Figure 2.4 shows several commercially available geoboards.

By stretching rubber bands over the pegs or nails on a geoboard, it is possible to make numerous geometric shapes. Generally, regardless of the actual length between the equally spaced pegs or nails, this distance is referred to as one unit. Therefore, the squares on the geoboards at the bottom of Figure 2.4 both have an area of 4 square units since each square has a side length of 2 units.

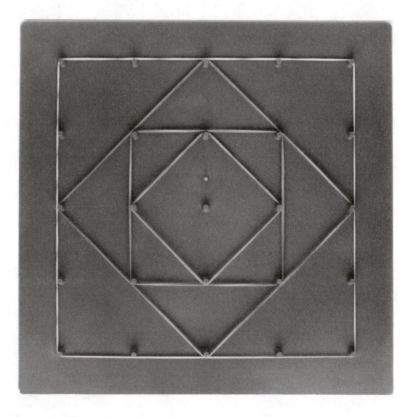

Figure 2.4   Geoboard

Section E   Sequence of Activities

Identifying Triangles

Give each student a geoboard and 6 to 8 rubber bands. Ask students to make a triangle on the geoboard using one rubber band. Walk around the classroom and survey the triangles generated. Specifically, you are looking to see whether students are making three types of triangles—acute, with all angles less than 90 degrees, as illustrated in Figure 2.5; obtuse, with one angle greater than 90 degrees, as illustrated in Figure 2.6; and right, with one angle equal to 90 degrees as illustrated in Figure 2.7.

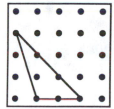
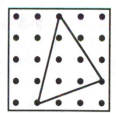
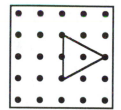

Figure 2.5   Acute Triangles

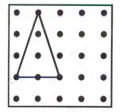
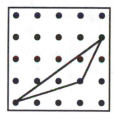
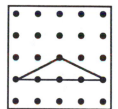

Figure 2.6   Obtuse Triangles

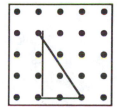
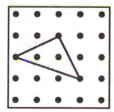
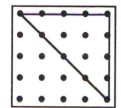

Figure 2.7   Right Triangles

(i) How do you decide whether a particular triangle not in standard position (i.e., with the base parallel to the top and bottom of the geoboard) is a right triangle? One way to do so is to rotate the triangle and compare it to a given right angle. If the angles are congruent, then the triangle is a right triangle. Also, if some transformational geometry has been developed with students, you might demonstrate how a right angle is its own supplement by reflecting the triangle along one of its sides.

As you walk around the room, look for several students who have formed right triangles. You will need at least three (four would be better) for the next phase of this activity. If not enough right triangles have been made by students, construct a few on geoboards of your own as you walk around the room.

After students have completed the "making triangles on a geoboard" task, tell them that they are going to play a game with you called "I'm Thinking of a Rule." Explain how the game is played by saying the following:

"I am thinking of a rule for separating your geoboards into two (2) groups. One of the groups will be on this table [point to the appropriate location], and the other group will be on that table there [point to another appropriate location]. I want you to guess my rule, and I will give you clues as we play."

Then ask one of the students who has a right triangle to come forward and place the geoboard on one of the tables. Say to the students,

"We will call geoboards on this table the A Group."

Put the place card with the words "The A Group" on the table. It is important that you not reveal to students that the A Group will have geoboards with right triangles, because this is the rule you want them to discover.

Next, ask any student to come forward with a geoboard. Look at the geoboard and determine whether or not the triangle is a right triangle. If it is a right triangle, place it on the A Group table. Tell students,

"This geoboard belongs in the A Group."

If it is not a right triangle, place it on the other table and say to the students,

> "This geoboard does not belong in the A Group. I am going to put it on the other table. We will call this the Not A Group."

Also, put the place card with the words "The Not A Group" on the appropriate table.

Continue inviting students to come forward. Each time, determine whether or not their triangle is a right triangle, and place the triangle on the appropriate table. Each time you place a geoboard on a table, say to the class either

> "This geoboard is in the A Group"

or

> "This geoboard is in the Not A Group,"

whichever is the appropriate statement.

Once several geoboards have been placed (say, two in one group and three in another), you can vary the routine slightly to engage students even more in the activity. When the next student comes forward, ask the class,

> "On which table do you think the geoboard should be placed?"

Select a student to answer and ask the others if they agree. If there is general agreement and the class is correct, direct the student to place the geoboard on the appropriate table. If there is no agreement or the class has arrived at an incorrect conclusion, take the geoboard and say,

> "Well, actually, the geoboard belongs in the A Group,"

or

> "Well, actually, the geoboard belongs in the Not A Group,"

whichever is appropriate. Then place the geoboard on the appropriate table or direct a student to do so.

> *(ii) Whenever I do this activity, I like to give students a lot of positive reinforcement and encouragement to build their confidence and motivate their interest. Thus, when a student in the class correctly determines the group in which a particular geoboard belongs, I will make appropriate comments such as "Good work" or "Good thinking." When students are unable to determine or agree on the correct group, I still offer encouraging comments such as "Maybe we don't have enough information yet," or "Good try, let's see if we can all agree on the next one.*

When 8 or 9 geoboards have been placed on the tables, with at least 4 in the A Group, move to the next phase of the activity. Ask students,

> "What is the rule I am thinking of that determines the placement of the geoboards?"

You are, of course, looking for students to describe the common characteristics of the triangles in the A Group. These characteristics are:

1. Three sides

2. Three angles

3. One right angle

In this way you can motivate or review the definition of a right triangle. But the major purpose of this activity in the exploration is not to define right triangles. Rather, it is to have students identify, in a participatory rather than a "telling" way, that right triangles are the geometric shapes to be used for the next activity in the exploration.

By playing the "I'm Thinking of a Rule" game and reviewing the definition for a right triangle on a geoboard, readiness is established for moving on to the next activity in the exploration of the Pythagorean theorem.

(iii) One of the nice things about this activity is that it permits you to give (or review) the definition of a right triangle in a participatory way rather than in a "telling" way. There are two advantages of using such an approach. First, the type of thinking students use in the "I'm Thinking of a Rule" activity helps them develop the critical thinking and problem-solving skills so important in doing mathematics successfully. Second, when we try to tell students the definition of a term, frequently they are confused and have little in-depth feeling or understanding for the attributes or characteristics that establish the definition. As a result, they often have trouble remembering the definition. In contrast, when we design participatory experiences that engage students in generating and distinguishing identifying features or properties for themselves, they often determine the defining characteristics relatively easily. Frequently this leads to a clearer understanding of the definition and enables them to improve it in the future.

(iv) If your students are very young children, it may be necessary for you to guide them in the direction of looking for similarities and differences in the properties of the triangles in the A Group and the Not A Group in order to motivate the definition of a right triangle. One good way to do so is to ask students (or quickly review yourself) the general features of a triangle. Usually, when students remember or are introduced to the fact that a triangle has (a) three sides and (b) three angles, this information is sufficient to focus their attention on looking for side or angle relationships.

(v) In this phase of the activity we used the game "I'm Thinking of a Rule" to review or introduce the definition of a right triangle on a geoboard. This same "I'm Thinking of a Rule" game can also be used to review or introduce the definition of acute and obtuse triangles. Also, the game can be useful whenever you want to engage students in a participatory, discovery-type activity to establish a definition by determining the defining attributes or characteristics.

Defining Noncongruent Triangles

Tell students to clear their geoboards. Then ask them to make a right triangle on their geoboard. Walk around the room and select two specific right triangles to place on a table with the placecard that says "The A Group." In selecting the two right triangles, choose one with a base of 1 unit and a height (altitude) of 2 units, and another with a base of 2 units and a height (altitude) of 3 units. Two such triangles are shown in Figure 2.8. (*Note:* Hereafter, the words *height* and *altitude* will be used interchangeably.)

(i) If one of the required triangles has not been made by students, you can form the right triangle on one of your geoboards and place it on the A Group table. In fact, this technique is valuable at any point in the activity if students have not generated the desired triangles.

 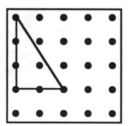

Figure 2.8   The A Group

Once the two geoboards are placed on a table, walk around the room and select two more right triangles to place, this time, on a table with the place card reading "The Not A Group." In selecting these two right triangles, again choose one with a base of 1 unit and a height of 2 units, and another with a base of 2 units and a height of 3 units. This time, however, take care to select right triangles that are located in different positions on the geoboard from the two triangles previously selected. For example, you might select the right triangles shown in Figure 2.9. Each has the same dimensions as the ones in the A Group but is located in a different position from those pictured in Figure 2.8.

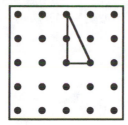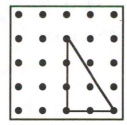

Figure 2.9   The Not A Group

Then, walk around the room and select two more specific right triangles to place on the table with the place card "The Not A Group." Again choose one right triangle with a base of 1 unit and a height of 2 units and another right triangle with a base of 2 units and a height of 3 units. But when you select or place these additional right triangles in the Not A Group, be very careful to arrange them in such a way that the orientation of the newly added right triangles is different from the orientation of those in the A Group. For example, you might place the two added geoboards in the Not A Group as shown in Figure 2.10.

Next, tell students that you are now going to play a version of

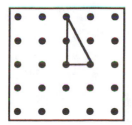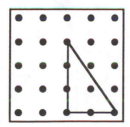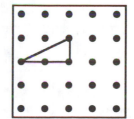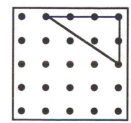

Figure 2.10   The Not A Group

the "I'm Thinking of a Rule" game with them. Point out that you are using a new rule (i.e., different than in the previous game) for placing the geoboards in the A and Not A Groups.

Then, select any student geoboard that has a right triangle with the same base and height dimensions as one of those already chosen (i.e., the triangles with a base of 1 or a base of 2 and a height of 3). Pay no attention to the orientation or the location of the triangle; any orientation or location will do. For example, you might select a right triangle with a base of 2 and a height of 3 units.

Now ask the class,

> "In which group does this right triangle belong—in the A Group or the Not A Group?" (*Answer:* It belongs in the Not A Group.)

If one or more students say,

> "It goes in the Not A Group,"

respond by saying,

> "Yes, it does,"

and place the geoboard in the Not A Group. If none of the students say,

> "It goes in the Not A Group,"

place it in the Not A Group and tell the class that this is the correct group for the right triangle. But *do not* say why it is the correct group.

Figure 2.11 illustrates the addition of the fifth right triangle to the Not A Group.

Next, select another student geoboard, this time for the A

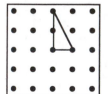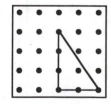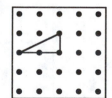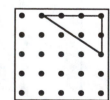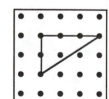

Figure 2.11   The Not A Group

Group. Choose one that has different base and height dimensions from either of the two right triangles in the A Group. For example, you might choose a geoboard with a base of 3 units and a height of 4 units, as shown in Figure 2.12.

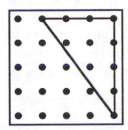

Figure 2.12   An A Group Right Triangle

Ask the class,

"According to my rule, which group does this right triangle belong to, the A Group or the Not A Group?" (*Answer:* The triangle belongs to the A Group.)

By design, the right triangle in Figure 2.12 properly belongs to the A Group. As a result of student responses or your own statement, you should place the geoboard in the A Group. At this point in the activity there is sufficient information for you to ask students if they can explain the rule you are using to separate the right triangles into the A Group and the Not A Group.

With proper guidance from you in terms of the questions you ask or the hints you provide, one or more students usually will have noticed that none of the triangles in the A Group have the same base and height. In other words, no triangle in the A Group is the same size as (congruent with) another triangle in the A Group.

A good way to end this phase of the activity is to review with students (or even ask them to explain) the rule you are using to place the geoboards in the A or the Not A Group. The rule can be described along the following lines.

1. A right triangle is selected.

2. The triangle has certain base and height dimensions.

3. If the A Group already has a right triangle with those base and height dimensions, place the right triangle in the Not A Group.

4. If the A Group does not have a right triangle with those base and height dimensions, place the right triangle in the A Group.

In other words, the rule for separating the right triangles places in the A Group one of each of the noncongruent right triangles that can be made on a geoboard. In the Not A Group the rule places right triangles that are congruent to those in the A Group. This particular distinction between congruent and noncongruent right triangles is important to the next activity in the exploration of the Pythagorean theorem.

(i) In this phase of the activity you could digress and discuss or develop for students the ideas of translating, rotating, and reflecting various geometric figures. These are motions (or operations) in transformational geometry that preserve the dimensions (length, width, perimeter, area, and volume) while changing the location or position of the figure. Often in the elementary grades these motions are referred to as slides, turns, and flips.

(ii) To some teachers, the development presented here on determining which right triangles to count will seem to require too much time to be justifiable. Depending on individual circumstances, this may, of course, be the case, and some teachers will prefer to skip this stage of the activity and merely tell students in the next stage to count only noncongruent right triangles.

It is important to note, however, that teachers employing a discovery method of teaching must constantly make judgments about the primary goals of an activity, what sequence of activities to include to reach the goals, how long to devote to a particular development, when a digression is warranted or worth devoting time to, how to adjust the lesson if the goals are not being achieved, and so on. The complete development in this section is presented to provide additional insight at the extreme on how the discovery method can be used to motivate the Pythagorean theorem.

Counting Right Triangles

For this activity in the exploration, it is a good idea to let students work in pairs or small groups. Each group will need two sheets of

5 × 5 geoboard grids, one geoboard, and 6–8 rubber bands for each student.

Instruct students to find all the different (noncongruent) right triangles they can make on the geoboard. Tell students to copy each different right triangle they find onto one of the 5 × 5 geoboard grid sheets. Allow sufficient time for students to explore this problem, and encourage them to work in small groups.

Surprisingly, there are 17 different (noncongruent) right triangles that can be formed on the geoboard. These are given in Figure 2.13.

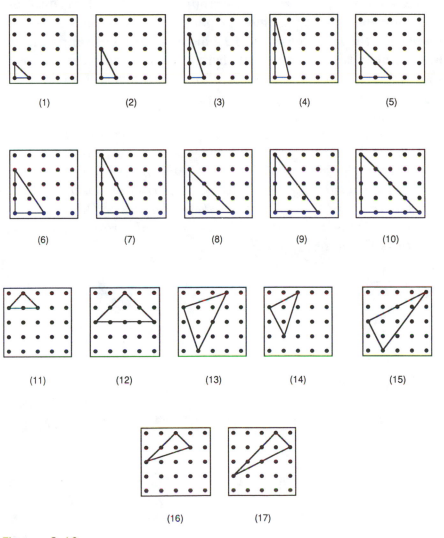

Figure 2.13

Often, even when students are permitted to work in small groups, they are not able to find all 17 of the different (noncongruent) right triangles that can be formed on the geoboard. Here is one technique for showing the class all of the 17 right triangles.

Tell students to place one right triangle on their geoboards. Walk around the room and select several students to place their geoboards in a group on the chalkboard tray or on a table. Be careful to choose noncongruent triangles to place on the chalkboard tray. Then ask,

"Who in class has a different triangle?"

Keep adding geoboards to the group until all 17 of the different (noncongruent) right triangles are placed or no new ones are volunteered. In the latter case, if all 17 have not yet been formed, you may want to tell students that there are some additional different right triangles and give them time to see if they can find the missing ones.

(i) To avoid possible confusion, you may want to stipulate in this activity that all the vertices of a triangle must touch a peg on the geoboard. Otherwise, you might have some students considering the types of right triangles illustrated by triangle ABC shown in Figure 2.14. For this exploration, such right triangles are not to be counted. Only triangles with vertices touching pegs will be used.

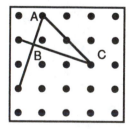

Figure 2.14   Type of Right Triangle Not to Be Counted

(ii) Depending on the students' age, their degree of sophistication, and their level of interest in the problem being explored, it may be helpful at some point to tell them exactly how many right triangles remain to be found, or to give suggestions such as ". . . change your point of view . . . ," or ". . . consider right triangles whose base and height are not parallel to the edges

of the geoboard. . . ." If necessary, of course, you may need to make any missing right triangles and show them to the class to complete the set of 17 given in Figure 2.13.

Building Squares

When all 17 of the different (noncongruent) right triangles have been constructed by students, place 4 geoboards with no figures on them on a table. This effectively forms a 10×10 geoboard as shown in Figure 2.15. Then construct the specific right triangle with base 2 and height 3, as shown in Figure 2.16.

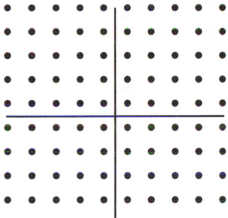

Figure 2.15

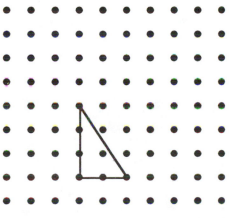

Figure 2.16

Invite students to gather around the table on which the 10 × 10 geoboard has been placed. Then place a rubber band as shown in Figure 2.17 to form a square along the base of the right triangle. Point to the square and ask students,

"What type of shape is this?" (*Answer:* The shape is a square.)

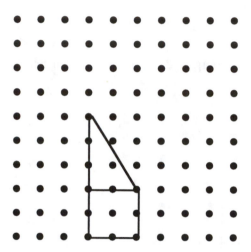

Figure 2.17

Next, ask students,

"What is the area of the square?" (*Answer:* The area is 4 square units.)

Show students how the area can easily be determined using rubber bands and counting the unit squares (see Figure 2.18).

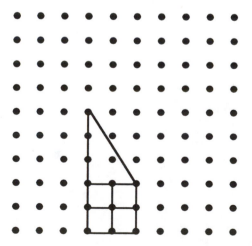

Figure 2.18

Then, place a rubber band as shown in Figure 2.19 to form a square along the height of the right triangle. Point to the square along the height and ask students,

"What type of shape is this?" (*Answer:* The shape is a square.)

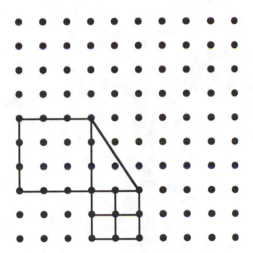

Figure 2.19

Next, ask students,

"What is the area of the square?" (*Answer:* The area is 9 square units.)

Show students how the area can be determined using rubber bands by counting the unit squares (see Figure 2.20).

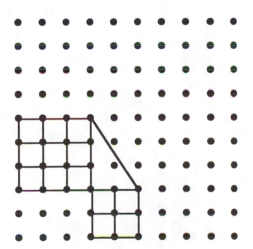

Figure 2.20

Finally, place a rubber band as shown in Figure 2.21 to form a square along the hypotenuse of the right triangle. Point to the square along the hypotenuse and ask students,

"What type of shape is this?" (*Answer:* The shape is a square.)

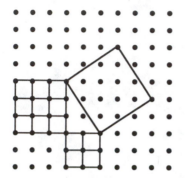

Figure 2.21

Next, ask students,

"How can you show the area of the square just formed using rubber bands?"

Pause a few moments to give students time to think about the answer. Then ask,

"Who knows and can tell me the area?" (*Answer:* The area is 13 square units.)

If a student claims to know the answer, invite that student to explain to the class how it can be done. If no student is able to tell you the area, you can demonstrate a method of finding it by placing rubber bands as shown in Figure 2.22 and counting the 13 unit squares.

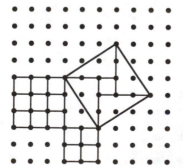

Figure 2.22

Here, depending on the background of your students, you may find it beneficial to show in greater detail that the area of the square along the hypotenuse is 13 square units. To do so, take four additional geoboards to form a 10 × 10 geoboard. Copy the square along the hypotenuse onto the new 10 × 10 geoboard, and form a rectangle with a rubber band as shown in Figure 2.23.

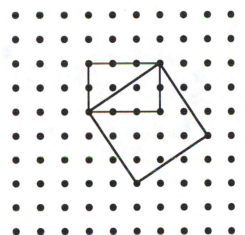

Figure 2.23

Point to the rectangle and count the unit squares inside the rectangle to show that the area of the rectangle is 6 square units. Note that the edge of the square (inside the rectangle) is a diagonal of the rectangle. To engage students actively, you might say to them at this point,

"The diagonal separates the rectangle into two pieces? What can you tell me about these pieces?"

Here the goal is for students to conclude that the diagonal separates the rectangle into two equal (congruent) right triangles. Because the two right triangles are equal (congruent), they have the same area. Since the area of the rectangle is 6 square units, the area of each triangle is 3 square units. Therefore, the area of the triangle inside the square (see the shaded region in Figure 2.24) is 3 square units.

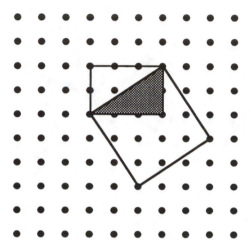

Figure 2.24

Returning to Figure 2.22, this line of reasoning verifies that the area of each of the four right triangles, inside the square along the hypotenuse, is 3 square units for a total of $4 \times 3 = 12$ square units of area. If you add this to the one square unit of area for the small square inside the square along the hypotenuse, you get an area of $12 + 1 = 13$ square units as the area of the square along the hypotenuse.

(i) This is an important activity in the motivational development and exploration of the Pythagorean theorem. Unfortunately, the standard inexpensive plastic 5 × 5 geoboards often found in schools cannot be used for this activity because they are not manufactured in such a way as to permit four of them to be placed together to form a uniform 10 × 10 geoboard. However, the standard 5 × 5 wood geoboards available from many suppliers are manufactured in such a way that when four are placed together they form a uniform 10 × 10

geoboard. Thus, it is preferable to use the wood geoboards in most classroom situations.

If necessary, you can do much of this activity with a demonstration technique before the whole class. This would permit you to do so with a limited supply of the appropriate 5 × 5 geoboards.

Some teachers have done this activity in the exploration solely on 10 × 10 dot paper. However, I have found it far more effective to use a 10 × 10 geoboard with students first. Developing the concept first with the concrete manipulative gives students a deeper understanding of the underlying ideas being studied.

(ii) With many students, it is helpful to show them in some way that the shape formed along the hypotenuse is, indeed, a square. For example, you can use the corner of a sheet of paper to show that each of the four angles is a right angle, mark off the length of one side on the paper, and show that the other sides are equal in length. Some students will see the shape immediately as a square, but many will not, simply because the sides of the square are not parallel to the edges of the geoboard. Because some students have difficulty recognizing geometric shapes in what they consider to be unusual (not typical) positions, taking time to verify that the shape is a square helps these students. Doing so also gives them experience with the problem-solving strategy known as "change your point of view."

(iii) A colleague, Dr. Klaus Fischer, associate professor of mathematics at George Mason University, suggests that Pick's theorem is an ideal way to compute the area of squares in this activity. Pick's theorem enables you to find the area, A, of any shape on a geoboard from the formula

$$A = \tfrac{1}{2}(O) + I - 1$$

where A is the area of the shape, O is the number of nails on the shape, and I is the number of nails in the interior of the shape. As Dr. Fischer points out, ". . . computing the area of the square along the hypotenuse is not easy. Your way of doing so is instructive but a little bit hard to follow for youngsters."

Because I have not previously used Pick's theorem with

adults to find the areas of the squares in the development in this activity, I have not incorporated Dr. Fischer's suggestion here. However, his idea is of sufficient interest and merit that I include it here so interested teachers might experiment with developing a discovery-oriented method for using Pick's theorem to compute areas in this activity.

Generating Data

For this phase of the exploration, have students return to their small groups and form a 10 × 10 geoboard. While students are doing so, you should physically separate the 17 geoboards obtained in the previous activity with the right triangles into two groups; one group with 11 geoboards, the other group with 6 geoboards. The two groupings are shown in Figure 2.25 and Figure 2.26.

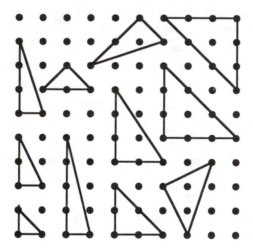

Figure 2.25   The Group of 11 Geoboards

The 11 geoboards in Figure 2.25 show the right triangles to be used in this activity. They are the right triangles that can be placed somewhere on the 10 × 10 geoboard so that sufficient space remains to permit squares to be formed on the base, the height, and the hypotenuse. To do so with the 6 right triangles shown in Figure 2.26 would require a geoboard larger than 10 × 10. In fact, to show each of the 6, you would need a 13 × 13 geoboard.

Notice that 7 of the right triangles in Figure 2.25 have two sides that are parallel to the edges of the geoboard. These are shown in

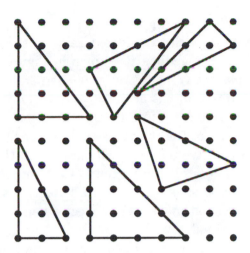

Figure 2.26   The Group of 6 Geoboards

Figure 2.27. Four of the right triangles in Figure 2.25 have at most one side parallel to the edges of the geoboard (i.e., zero or one side parallel to the edges of the geoboard). These 4 right triangles are shown in Figure 2.28.

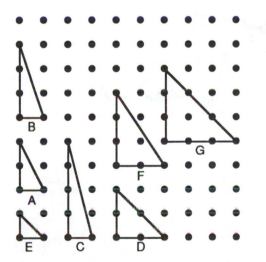

Figure 2.27   Right Triangles with Two Sides Parallel to the Edges of the Geoboard

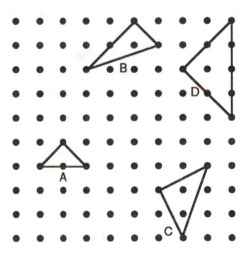

Figure 2.28   Right Triangles with at Most One Side Parallel to the Edges of the Geoboard

Now, give each group of students one of the 4 geoboards that has a right triangle with two sides parallel to the edges of the geoboard. These are the geoboards shown in Figure 2.27. You might use, for example, the right triangles labeled A, B, C, and D in Figure 2.27. This phase of the activity works well with four or more groups. If you use exactly four groups, give each group a different geoboard with one of the triangles A, B, C, or D. If you use more than four groups, give out the geoboards with the right triangles A, B, C, and D, but tell some groups that they will be using the same right triangle as another group. Effectively, this provides a check for the data students will collect when you give them the task to be performed.

When each group has a geoboard containing one of the 4 right triangles with two sides parallel to the edges of the geoboard (those labeled A, B, C, and D in Figure 2.27), give the following directions. Tell students to copy the right triangle onto their 10 × 10 geoboard. Tell them to place the triangle in the 10 × 10 geoboard in such a way that sufficient space is left to form a square along each side of the triangle. Reinforce this latter point by telling students they may find it necessary to move the right triangle once they start forming the squares. This will be necessary if a side of a square they are trying to form along a side of the triangle falls off the geoboard. In other words, tell them you want the right triangle and each of the squares formed along the three sides of the triangle to be formed completely on the 10 × 10 geoboard.

Walk around the room and observe the students' work. As individual groups complete forming the squares along the sides of the triangles, tell them to determine the area of each square. Direct students to show with rubber bands how they might verify that the area obtained is the correct area.

Continue walking around the room to observe student work. As they discover and verify the areas, instruct them to copy the right triangle and each of the three squares along the sides of the triangle onto one of the 10 × 10 dot arrays on the grid sheet. But tell students not to indicate (or show) the area of the three squares by drawing lines. Instead, have them write the area inside each square as illustrated in Figure 2.29.

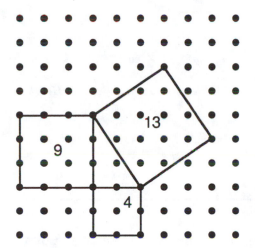

Figure 2.29

(i) This activity in the exploration to motivate the Pythagorean theorem is important because it sets the stage for collecting and presenting sufficient data to enable students to determine the Pythagorean relationship by observing the data and looking for patterns. My own experience suggests that most students must see at least four cases of the generalization in order to form a hypothesis about the relationship. However, many students need to see five or even more cases in order to have enough information to formulate a hypothesis about the relationship.

Collecting Data

After each group has completed the previous task for the right triangle assigned, go to the blackboard and write the column headings for a table of data as given in Table 2.1.

TABLE 2.1   Areas of Squares

Length of Base of Triangle	Length of Height of Triangle	Area of Square on Base	Area of Square on Height	Area of Square on Hypotenuse

39

Then ask each group in turn to report the data they collected, and record that data in the appropriate columns. For this activity it is not necessary to collect the data in any organized or systematic fashion. In fact, it may be more effective to collect and record the data in what might appear to be a random fashion, as illustrated in Table 2.2.

TABLE 2.2   Areas of Squares

Length of Base of Triangle	Length of Height of Triangle	Area of Square on Base	Area of Square on Height	Area of Square on Hypotenuse
1	4	1	16	17
2	2	4	4	8
1	2	1	4	5
1	3	1	9	10
2	3	4	9	13

As the last entry in the table at this point (i.e., the fifth row), record the data from the right triangle in Figure 2.29 that you used to initiate the construction of squares activity. Remind students that this is the source of the data.

(i) Once you complete the entire exploration of the Pythagorean theorem presented in this chapter, it will be valuable to revisit the original problem and the various activities used to develop the solution. In this revisitation step you should reexamine the problem, the solution strategies used to solve the problem, the various problem-solving steps employed, any mathematical concepts covered, insights gained, and so on. The activity in this part of the exploration, during such a revisitation, can be used as a good example for students to illustrate the important role that tables, graphs, and charts play in problem solving. I particularly like to point out in reviewing this part of the exploration that by presenting the data that lead to the Pythagorean theorem in tabular form, instructors increase the likelihood that many students will be able to analyze the data, see patterns, and form a hypothesis. If the data were not presented in a table or in some other organized way, many students would fail to arrive at any meaningful conclusion from the experience.

Looking for Patterns

Now ask students to examine the data in Table 2.2. The object here is for them to look for and report any interesting patterns. Provide ample time for thought and then give students an opportunity to describe any patterns they might have discovered.

Depending on their sophistication, students will usually observe and be able to describe several different patterns from the data. Some of the patterns described more frequently include the following:

1. Numbers in the first column are always 1 or 2.

2. Numbers in the second column are less than 5.

3. Numbers in the third and fourth columns are perfect squares.

4. Numbers in the third column are the square of the corresponding number in the first column.

5. Numbers in the fourth column are the square of the corresponding number in the second column.

6. Numbers in the fifth column are the sum of the corresponding numbers in the third and fourth columns.

The objective in this stage of the activity is to guide students to observation 6. Specifically, you want students to recognize on their own, if possible, that the area of the square on the hypotenuse is the sum of the area of the square on the base and the area of the square on the height. At this point, however, it is not necessary to verbalize it in this way.

Conclude this stage of the activity by considering the right triangles labeled E and G in Figure 2.27. Take the geoboard with the right triangle labeled E and hold it up for students to view. Then go to the board to enter a sixth line of data, as shown in Table 2.3. Gather and record the data column by column by asking students the following questions. In each case point to the referenced segment or outline it with your finger, but do not construct or form the squares with rubber bands. At this point, you want students to visualize the squares without actually seeing them in place.

TABLE 2.3 Areas of Squares

Length of Base of Triangle	Length of Height of Triangle	Area of Square on Base	Area of Square on Height	Area of Square on Hypotenuse
1	4	1	16	17
2	2	4	4	8
1	2	1	4	5
1	3	1	9	10
2	3	4	9	13
1	1	1	1	2

1. "What is the length of the base?" Point to the base. (*Answer:* The length of the base is 1 unit.)

2. "What is the length of the height?" Point to the height." (*Answer:* The length of the height is 1 unit.)

3. "What is the area of the square on the base?" Run your finger along the outline of the square on the base. (*Answer:* The area of the square is 1 square unit.)

4. "What is the area of the square on the height?" Run your finger along the outline of the square on the height. (*Answer:* The area of the square is 1 square unit.)

5. "What is the area of the square on the hypotenuse?" Run your finger along the outline of the square on the hypotenuse. (*Answer:* The area of the square is 2 square units.)

Finally, take the geoboard with the right triangle labeled (G) in Figure 2.27. Hold the geoboard for all to see and ask the following series of questions. Record the data in the table as shown in Table 2.4.

TABLE 2.4   Areas of Squares

Length of Base of Triangle	Length of Height of Triangle	Area of Square on Base	Area of Square on Height	Area of Square on Hypotenuse
1	4	1	16	17
2	2	4	4	8
1	2	1	4	5
1	3	1	9	10
2	3	4	9	13
1	1	1	1	2
3	3	9	9	18

1. "What is the length of the base?" Point to the base. (*Answer:* The length of the base is 3 units.)

2. "What is the length of the height?" Point to the height. (*Answer:* The length of the height is 3 units.)

3. "What is the area of the square on the base?" Run your finger along the outline of the square on the base. (*Answer:* The area of the square is 9 square units.)

4. "What is the area of the square on the height?" Run your finger along the outline of the square on the height. (*Answer:* The area of the square is 9 square units.)

5. "What is the area of the square on the hypotenuse?" Run your finger along the outline of the square on the hypotenuse. (*Answer:* The area of the square is 18 square units.)

A good way to conclude this activity is to have students copy the right triangle labeled G from Figure 2.27 onto one of their 10 × 10 dot grids before you ask the foregoing questions and collect the data. Once they copy the triangle, ask them to do the following:

1. Draw the squares on the base, the height, and the hypotenuse.

2. Show by drawing lines how they could determine the areas of the three squares.

3. Verify that, indeed, the area of the square on the hypotenuse, 18 square units, equals the sum of the area of the square on the base, 9 square units, plus the area of the square on the height, 9 square units.

By following these three steps, students review the major ideas studied. This also gives you an informal opportunity to assess student concept development to this point.

(i) When students look for patterns and observe the relationship that the area of the square on the hypotenuse is the sum of the area of the square on the base and the area of the square on the height, they have effectively formed a generalization from the data presented for several cases. At this point the generalization is actually a hypothesis. It is important for students to test and verify that the hypothesis is a correct one. In adding data to the table for the right triangles labeled E and G in Figure 2.27 students are helping to verify that the hypothesis appears to be true.

Generalizing the Result and Stating the Conclusion

At this stage of the exploration, move to the blackboard and draw a right triangle with the base labeled 3 and the height labeled 5, as shown in Figure 2.30.

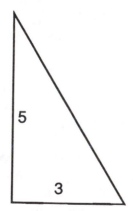

Figure 2.30

Ask students:

"Imagine a square on the base. What is the area of the square?" (*Answer:* The area of the square is 9 square units).

44

Then sketch the square as shown in Figure 2.31. Record the area of the square, 9, inside the square. Ask students:

"Imagine a square on the height. What is the area of the square?" (*Answer:* The area of the square is 25 square units.)

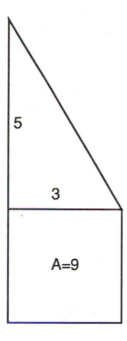

Figure 2.31

Then sketch the square as shown in Figure 2.32. Record the area of 25 square units inside the square. Ask students:

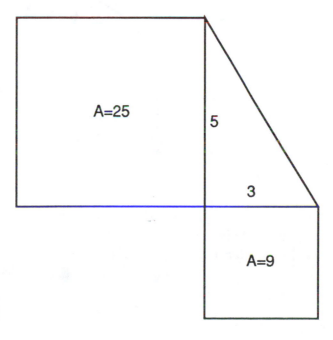

Figure 2.32

"Imagine a square on the hypotenuse. What is the area of the square?" (*Answer:* The area of the square is 34 square units.)

Then sketch the square as shown in Figure 2.33. Record the area of 34 square units inside the square.

In order to reinforce the ideas developed in this activity, it is valuable to select several more right triangles and walk students through the sequence of steps above. Three such triangles are shown in Figures 2.34, 2.35, and 2.36. Draw each of these on the blackboard for students to see.

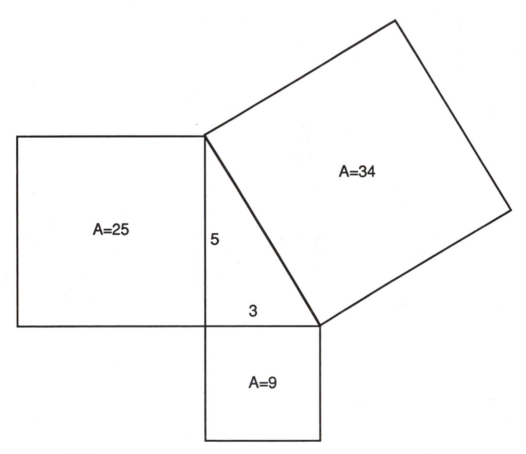

Figure 2.33

Next, draw a right triangle on the blackboard and label the base "a" and the height "b" as shown in Figure 2.37.

Guide students through the following sequence of questions.

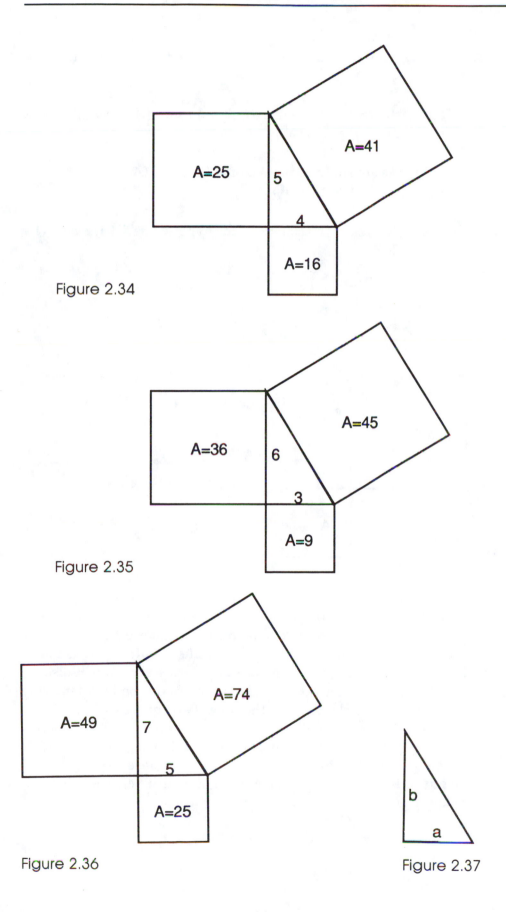

Figure 2.34

Figure 2.35

Figure 2.36

Figure 2.37

Record the answers on the blackboard in turn as shown in Figure 2.38.

1. "What is the area of the square on the base?" (*Answer:* The area of the square is a × a or a².)

2. "What is the area of the square on the height?" (*Answer:* The area of the square is b × b or b².)

3. "What is the area of the square on the hypotenuse?" (*Answer:* The area is a² + b².)

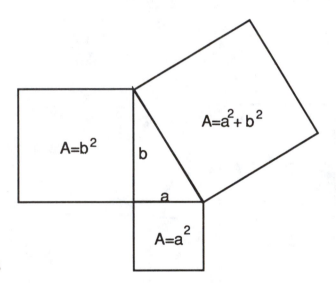

Figure 2.38

By now, most students will be able to explain that the area of the square on the base, a × a, is found by squaring the length of the base, and the area of the square on the height, b × b, is found by squaring the length of the height. Most students will also be able to conclude that the area of the square on the hypotenuse is found by adding the areas of the other two squares.

At this stage students have been motivated through a series of participatory activities to discover the Pythagorean theorem, which states that, for a right triangle with base of length "a," height of length "b," and hypotenuse of length "c," the following holds true:

$$a^2 + b^2 = c^2$$

(i) By this stage of the exploration, most students are ready for the statement of the Pythagorean theorem in the form $a^2 + b^2 = c^2$. The concrete, hands-on development makes the formula much less abstract to students. Students are literally able to "see" the formula as areas of squares, and the symbols take on specific meaning because they relate back to the squares most students are now able to visualize. In fact, it is useful to review with students that the relationship $a^2 + b^2 = c^2$ actually describes a very real situation—namely, that a right triangle with base "a" and height "b" can have squares along the base and height with areas of a^2 and b^2, respectively, and that the sum of these squares, $a^2 + b^2$, gives the area of the square along the hypotenuse, which we call c^2.

Solving the Problem

The Pythagorean theorem exploration leads quite nicely to students discovering irrational numbers. Once the development is completed and summarized by the statement that the area of the square on the hypotenuse of a right triangle equals the sum of the areas of the squares on the base and height, (i.e., $a^2 + b^2 = c^2$), students are ready to consider the original problem given at the beginning of this chapter: What is the length of the hypotenuse for the right triangle with base equal to 5 units and height equal to 7 units?

One method for leading students to the correct result is to select several specific cases involving other right triangles and to have students explain how they might find the area of the square on the hypotenuse. For example, consider the triangle with base 3 and height 5 in Figure 2.33. In that case, the area of the square on the base is 9, the area of the square on the height is 25, and the area of the square on the hypotenuse is $9 + 25 = 34$. In other words,

$$3^2 + 5^2 = 9 + 25 = 34$$

Thus, the area of the square on the hypotenuse is 34.

By this point, most students have no difficulty understanding that the area of any square is found by squaring the length of one of the sides. You can use this fact by asking the question, "If a square has an area of 34 square units, what is the length of each side?"

Depending on your students' age and sophistication, you might want to branch out at this point in a number of possible directions, as appropriate. For students who have never studied irrational numbers, one simplistic way to introduce this topic to review briefly with students the table of squares shown in Table 2.5.

TABLE 2.5   Square Numbers

Integer	Square
1	$1 = 1 \times 1$
2	$4 = 2 \times 2$
3	$9 = 3 \times 3$
4	$16 = 4 \times 4$
5	$25 = 5 \times 5$
6	$36 = 6 \times 6$
7	$49 = 7 \times 7$
8	$64 = 8 \times 8$
9	$81 = 9 \times 9$
10	$100 = 10 \times 10$

Explain that the integers in column 2 are called perfect squares, and point out that the perfect squares are the squares of the integers in column 1. Then explain that a positive number whose square is equal to some number, called "n," is called the square root of "n." Thus, 2 is the square root of 4, since $2^2 = 4$. Here you should remind students of the relationship between the length of the side of a square and the area of the square and take care to point out, as an example, that if the area of a square is 9 square units, the length of the side of the square is the square root of 9, or 3 units.

Next ask students,

"If the area of a square is 34 square units, where would it belong in Table 2.5?"

Most students will respond with a statement like,

"Somewhere between 25 and 36 square units."

Then ask,

"What two numbers do you think the square root of 34 is between?" (*Answer:* The square root of 34 is between 5 and 6.)

Finally, tell students that the square root of 34 is written $\sqrt{34}$, and $34 = \sqrt{34} \times \sqrt{34}$.

To conclude this exploration and bring closure for students, you will want to answer the original problem given:

"In the triangle in Figure 2.1, what is the length of the third side?"

By this point, most students should be able to conclude that the length of the hypotenuse is $\sqrt{74}$, since $5^2 + 7^2 = 74$.

Section F   Extensions

Finding Irrational Lengths

Once students grasp the concept of determining the lengths of irrational segments, it is useful to reinforce all the ideas explored in this activity. One way to do so is to invite students to determine the lengths of all of the sides of each of the four right triangles that do not have two sides parallel to the edges of the geoboard. These right triangles have many sides that are of irrational lengths, as shown in Figure 2.28. The actual lengths of the sides are summarized here and given in Figure 2.39.

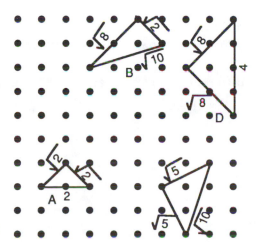

Figure 2.39

1. Triangle A has sides of lengths $\sqrt{2}$, 2, and $\sqrt{2}$.

2. Triangle B has sides of lengths $\sqrt{8}$, $\sqrt{2}$, and $\sqrt{10}$.

3. Triangle C has sides of lengths $\sqrt{5}$, $\sqrt{5}$, and $\sqrt{10}$.

4. Triangle D has sides of lengths $\sqrt{8}$, $\sqrt{8}$, and 4.

Extending the Pythagorean Relationship

Once the Pythagorean theorem has been developed, it is instructive for students to consider the following questions:

1. Does the relation $a^2 + b^2 = c^2$ hold for triangles that are not right triangles?

2. If a triangle is not a right triangle, is there a relationship between the sides? If so, what is the relationship?

Finding All Noncongruent Right Triangles on a Geoboard

Figure 2.14 shows an example of a right triangle on a 5×5 geoboard that does not have all of its three vertices on nails. This leads to a set of questions regarding the number of right triangles that can be constructed on a geoboard if it is a requirement that all of the vertices are on nails of the geoboard.

1. How many different (noncongruent) right triangles can be constructed on a 5×5 geoboard with exactly two vertices on nails?

2. How many different (noncongruent) right triangles can be constructed on a 5×5 geoboard with exactly one vertex on a nail?

3. How many different (noncongruent) right triangles can be constructed on a 5×5 geoboard with no vertices on a nail?

M O T I V A T I N G
Pascal's Triangle
with Cubes

CHAPTER CONTENTS

Section A   The Problem

Section B   Unit Objectives

Primary Objectives for This Exploration

Secondary Objectives for This Exploration

Section C   The Materials

Section D   Description of the Cubes

Section E   The Sequence of Activities

Defining the Problem
Initiating the Experiment
Collecting Additional Data
Recording the Data
Predicting the Next Case
Verifying the Prediction
Developing a General Method
Testing the General Method
Solving the Original Problem
Introducing Pascal's Triangle

Section F   Extensions

Generating the Triangular Numbers
Sums of Numbers in Pascal's
Triangle
Exploring Alternative Definitions

Activity Sheets

Section A   The Problem

What is the total number of different ways to stack 10 cubes in 1, 2, 3, . . . , 8, 9, 10 columns?

Section B   Unit Objectives

Primary Objectives for This Exploration

1. Experiencing the problem-solving steps: (1) understanding a problem, (2) devising a solution plan, (3) experimenting to collect data, (4) making and checking predictions from previous data, (5) forming and verifying a hypothesis, (6) organizing data systematically, (7) analyzing data, and (8) stating a conclusion.

2. Defining the word *different* in the question, "What is the total number of different ways to stack 10 cubes in 1, 2, 3, . . . , 8, 9, 10 columns?"

3. Showing that the sum of the entries of the nth row in Pascal's triangle is $y = 2^n - 1$, through a sequence of activities, as the solution of a specific problem motivated by the use of cubes.

4. Demonstrating how Pascal's triangle can be used as an aid in solving the problem of determining the number of different ways 10 cubes can be stacked in 1, 2, 3, . . . , 8, 9, 10 columns?"

Secondary Objectives for This Exploration

1. Exploring the properties of triangular numbers.

2. Developing a formula for the sum of n consecutive integers.

3. Determining alternative interpretations for the meaning of the phrase "number of different ways."

4. Stating generalizations from observed patterns of data in both tabular and pictorial representations.

Section C   The Materials

192 cubes for each student or group of students

1 copy of Activity Sheets 3.1, 3.2, 3.3, and 3.4 in the Activity Sheets section of this exploration for each student or group of students

(i) Groups of 4, 5, or 6 students can explore this problem. Thus, a class of 30 students, in groups of 6, would require 5 sets of 192 cubes, or a total of less than 1,000 cubes. If even this amount exceeds the resources of a classroom, the exploration can be done with 80 cubes for each of 5 groups, a total of 400 cubes for a class of 30 students, by slightly modifying the activity as noted in part 6 of Section E of this chapter, "Verifying the Prediction."

Section D   Description of the Cubes

There are basically two types of cubes—linking or nonlinking—that can be used for this exploration. Linking cubes, such as Multilink Cubes or Unifix Cubes, are constructed in such a way that they can be joined together or connected to build various three-dimensional structures. Figure 3.1 shows some Multilink Cubes. These cubes are usually made of plastic and measure 2 cm × 2 cm × 2 cm. Figure 3.2 shows some Unifix Cubes, which are also usually made of plastic.

Nonlinking cubes can also be used to build some three-dimensional structures, but they cannot be joined together except by the use of glue, tape, or some other adhesive. Instead, to build with nonlinking cubes, they must be stacked one on top of (or next to) another to form a desired structure. Figure 3.3 shows some typical nonlinking cubes. These cubes are usually made of wood and most frequently measure 1″ × 1″ × 1″ or 2 cm × 2 cm × 2 cm.

Some nonlinking cube sets contain cubes of a single color (e.g., all six faces are white, all six faces are natural wood, all six faces are black, etc.). Other nonlinking cube sets contain cubes of several colors. In such sets, some cubes will have all six faces of one color, some cubes will have six faces of another color, and so on.

Either linking or nonlinking cubes can be used in this exploration. Linking cubes have the advantage of forming rigid structures that students can lift and move easily, but nonlinking cubes allow you to build structures and take them apart more easily and quickly.

Figure 3.1   Multilink cubes.

Figure 3.2   Unifix cubes.

Figure 3.3   Color cubes.

Section E The Sequence of Activities

Defining the Problem

Place at least 128 cubes in a pile for each group of four students. Ask each student in the group to take 3 cubes and stack them in a single column. Most students will do so correctly, as shown in Figure 3.4.

Then take 3 cubes yourself and arrange them on a table in three separate stacks for all students to see, as shown in Figure 3.5. As you do so, tell the students,

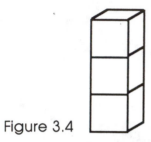

Figure 3.4

"This is the only way of stacking the 3 cubes in three columns."

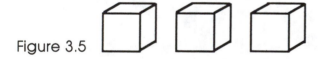

Figure 3.5

Now instruct students to find all of the different ways to stack 3 cubes in two columns. Tell them to construct each way of stacking the cubes in two columns and to place each of the ways they find on the table in front of them.

(i) For this problem it is a requirement that there must be at least one cube in each column. Instead of telling that to students, however, I usually find it valuable to let them begin the exploration without this clarification. Inevitably, the question

arises as to whether or not they should include the case with 3 cubes in one stack and 0 cubes in the other. When this question arises, it can be answered and provides a good opportunity to comment on the importance in problem solving of understanding the problem to be solved. In this instance, I like to point out to students that there are often several possible interpretations for a problem. Therefore, their first task in problem solving should be identifying the possible interpretations. The next task is to determine which of the interpretations makes the most sense for the context of the problem under exploration. Finally, I point out that in many cases they will have to make a reasoned judgment in determining for themselves which interpretation seems most appropriate. In those cases, they should always attempt to develop a rationale for the interpretation selected.

After sufficient time has passed for students to perform the task assigned, ask the question

"How many different ways did you find to stack the cubes in two columns?"

You should expect some students to say there are two ways to stack the 3 cubes in two columns. These students generally count the arrangement shown in Figure 3.6 and the arrangement shown in Figure 3.7 as different ways to stack the cubes. Some students, however, will say there is only one way to stack the cubes. They will be thinking of the two arrangements in Figures 3.6 and 3.7 as being the same.

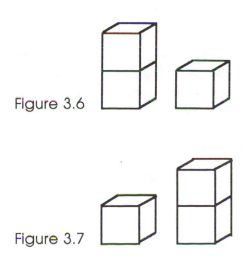

Figure 3.6

Figure 3.7

Depending on the students' age and mathematics background, it is a good idea to ask them which answer they think is correct. In other words, is there one or two different ways to stack 3 cubes in two columns?

Actually, both responses are "correct." Rotating the arrangement of cubes in either Figure 3.6 or Figure 3.7 gives the other arrangement. In that sense, both arrangements are equivalent, and there is only one way to stack the cubes in two columns. With this interpretation, the one way to stack the cubes is to have one column with 2 cubes and one column with 1 cube.

If, however, in determining what arrangements are different, you consider two factors—both the number of cubes and the placement of each column reading left to right—then there are two ways to stack the cubes. One way involves stacking the cubes so the column on the left has 2 cubes and the column on the right has 1 cube. The other way involves stacking the cubes so the column on the left has 1 cube and the column on the right has 2 cubes.

For this exploration, we will use the latter interpretation and say that there are two different ways to stack 3 cubes, as shown in Figure 3.8. Thus, to determine the different ways of stacking cubes in columns for this exploration, both the number of cubes and the placement of each column will be considered.

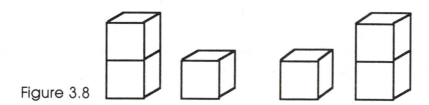

Figure 3.8

(i) Asking students to find and construct all the different ways to stack 3 cubes in two columns provides an activity-based way to define for them what is meant by "different" in this problem. Instead of telling or giving them the definition, using the approach described enables many students to discover for themselves the ways of stacking the cubes that are to be counted as different.

Initiating the Experiment

Distribute Activity Sheet 3.1 to students. It contains the information shown in Figure 3.9.

Take 4 cubes and show all the different ways you can stack them in one, two, three, and four columns. Record the number of different ways you found in the space provided in the table below.

Number of Columns	Number of Ways
1	_____
2	_____
3	_____
4	_____
Total	_____

FIGURE 3.9   ACTIVITY SHEET 3.1: Stacking 4 Cubes in Columns

Tell students that their task is to construct all of the different ways 4 cubes can be stacked in one, two, three, and four columns.

As students work, circulate around the room to see that they are on the right track. Provide assistance on a one-to-one basis to those who need help.

When sufficient time has passed for most students to complete the task, discuss with the class the answers obtained by various students.

A good technique for conducting the discussion is to ask individual students to tell the class how many ways they discovered to stack the 4 cubes. Begin the questioning by asking,

> "How many ways did you find to stack four (4) cubes in one (1) column?" (*Answer:* There is one way to stack 4 cubes in one column).

Then ask,

> "How many ways are there are to stack 4 cubes in four columns?" (*Answer:* There is one way to stack 4 cubes in four columns.)

The answers for these two cases are obvious, and no further discussion is needed.

Next, ask the question,

> "How many different ways did you discover to stack the

four (4) cubes in two (2) columns?" (*Answer:* There are three ways to stack 4 cubes in two columns.)

Now, in asking the question, the focus should be on having the student who provides the answer explain why the answer given is correct. A typical student response might go something like this:

"You must have two columns. So the most cubes you can have in the left column is 3. Then there will be 1 cube in the right column (see Figure 3.10). You can also have 2 cubes in the left column with 2 cubes in the right column (see Figure 3.11). Finally, you can have the left column with 1 cube and the right column with 3 cubes (see Figure 3.12). This gives a total of three ways to stack the 4 cubes."

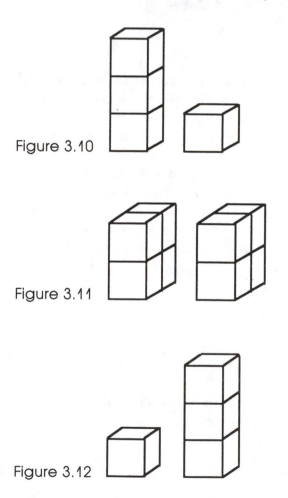

Figure 3.10

Figure 3.11

Figure 3.12

The typical student response given has been edited and refined for clarity. Student responses are rarely as straightforward or coherent as those in the preceding paragraph. Generally, students grasp the underlying concept and are able to present a line of reasoning that approximates the line of thought given. Usually, however, they lack the verbal skills needed to communicate their thinking to others. Therefore, you should be patient in listening to student explanations and be prepared to help them state a suitable rationale.

Similarly, you should ask for the number of different ways 4 cubes can be stacked in three columns. (*Answer:* There are a total of three ways to stack 4 cubes in three columns.) A typical student rationale explaining why there are a total of three ways to stack the cubes might go something like this:

> "There must be three columns. Each of these three columns has at least 1 cube. So the most cubes you can have in the leftmost column is 2, since there must be at least 1 cube in the remaining two columns (see Figure 3.13). And the most cubes you can have in the rightmost column is also 2, for the same reason (see Figure 3.14.) Also, the most cubes you can have in the middle column is 2, again for the same reason (see Figure 3.15). This gives a total of three ways for stacking 4 cubes in three columns."

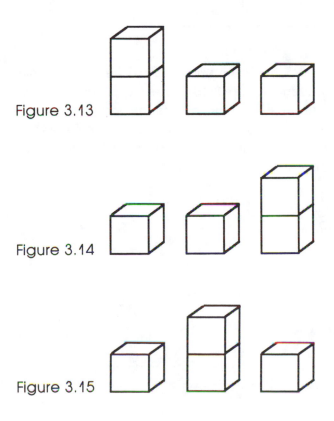

Figure 3.13

Figure 3.14

Figure 3.15

As students determine the number of ways of stacking the cubes, it is helpful for you to do two things. First, record the information on the blackboard as it is collected for all students in the class to see. Table 3.1 presents the table headings and initial piece of data that should be recorded. Second, as each new piece of data is obtained and recorded, actually construct each of the different ways the cubes can be stacked. Place them for all students to see. This insures that every student has an opportunity to verify personally that the number of different ways of stacking 4 cubes in two columns is, indeed, three, while the number of ways of stacking 4 cubes in three columns is also three.

TABLE 3.1   Number of Ways of Stacking 4 Cubes in Columns

Number of Columns	Number of Ways
1	1
2	—
3	—
4	—
Total	—

Figures 3.16 through 3.19 summarize the different ways of stacking 4 cubes in columns. Figure 3.16 shows the one way to stack the 4 cubes in one column. Figure 3.17 shows the one way to stack the 4 cubes in four columns. Figure 3.18 shows the three different ways to stack the 4 cubes in two columns, and Figure 3.19 shows the three different ways to stack the 4 cubes in three columns.

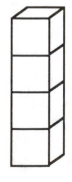

Figure 3.16

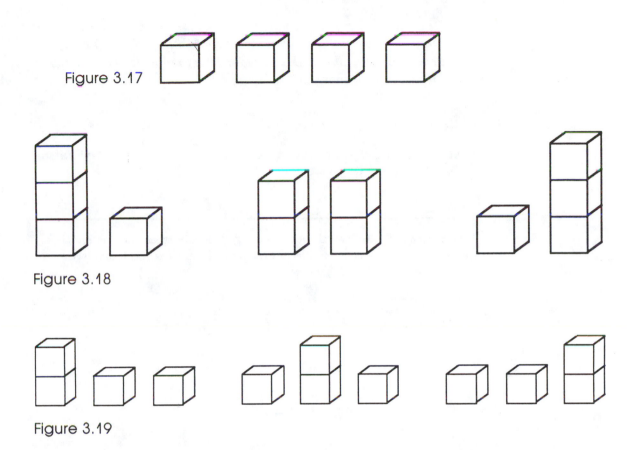

Figure 3.17

Figure 3.18

Figure 3.19

Table 3.2 summarizes the information on the different ways of stacking 4 cubes in one, two, three, and four columns as it would appear on your blackboard after all of the data have been collected and recorded.

TABLE 3.2 Number of Ways of Stacking 4 Cubes in Columns

Number of Columns	Number of Ways
1	1
2	3
3	3
4	1
Total	8

(i) *For your convenience, a copy of Activity Sheet 3.1 used in this section is included at the end of the chapter. You may repro-*

duce it for use in your own classroom. Similarly, copies of the other Activity Sheets described in this exploration are also provided for your own classroom use.

Collecting Additional Data

Distribute Activity Sheet 3.2 to students. It has the information shown in Figure 3.20.

Take 5 cubes and show all the different ways you can stack them in one, two, three, four, and five columns. Record the number of ways you found in the space provided in the table below.

Number of Columns	Number of Ways
1	_____
2	_____
3	_____
4	_____
5	_____
Total	_____

FIGURE 3.20   ACTIVITY SHEET 3.2: Stacking 5 Cubes in Columns

Direct students to construct all of the different ways to stack 5 cubes in one, two, three, four, and five columns. Depending on the number of cubes you have available, you may want to pair students for this part of the exploration or even have them work in groups of four or five. To construct all of the arrangements, a total of 80 cubes are required. Thus, for a class of 30 students you would need 2,400 cubes. If you pair the students, you would need a total of 1,200 cubes and, if you group the students by fours, you would only need a total of 600 cubes.

Circulate around the room while students are working and recording their data on the number of different ways of stacking 5 cubes on the activity sheet. Give help as required. When sufficient time has passed for most students to complete the task, ask students how many different ways they discovered. Record the answers on the board and construct all the arrangements for students to see. Doing this gives students a review of the correct ways of stacking 5 cubes in one, two, three, four, and five columns.

Figure 3.21 shows the one way of stacking 5 cubes in one column. Figure 3.22 shows the four ways of stacking 5 cubes in two columns. Figure 3.23 shows the six ways of stacking 5 cubes in three columns. Figure 3.24 shows the four ways of stacking 5 cubes in four columns. Figure 3.25 shows the one way of stacking 5 cubes in five

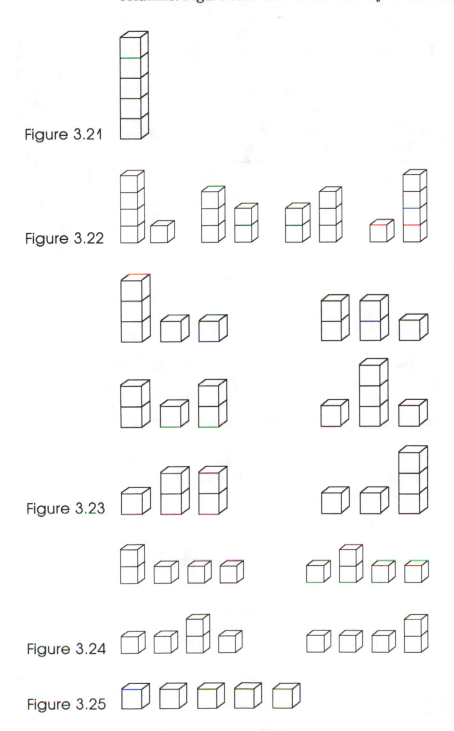

Figure 3.21

Figure 3.22

Figure 3.23

Figure 3.24

Figure 3.25

columns. Table 3.3 summarizes all the ways of stacking 5 cubes in one, two, three, four, and five columns and shows how that information would appear on the blackboard after you have recorded the data.

Recording the Data

Review for students the data that have been collected so far as recorded on the blackboard in the tables showing all the different ways both 4 and 5 cubes can be stacked in columns.

TABLE 3.3   Number of Ways of Stacking 5 Cubes in Columns

Number of Columns	Number of Ways
1	1
2	4
3	6
4	4
5	1
Total	16

Next, ask students to tell you, without actually constructing them, how many different ways they think there are to stack 3 cubes in one, two, and three columns. This will, of course, be a review since the "stacking cubes" activity began by finding the answer to this question. Many students will not remember the answer, and the exercise of thinking about the problem again will be useful.

From the student responses, make a table on the blackboard as shown in Table 3.4.

TABLE 3.4   Number of Ways of Stacking 3 Cubes in Columns

Number of Columns	Number of Ways
1	1
2	2
3	1
Total	4

Finally, ask students how many different ways are there to stack 1 cube and 2 cubes in columns. Record the information in tables on the blackboard as shown in Tables 3.5 and 3.6.

Make a point of showing students the actual arrangements of cubes in columns for these apparently obvious cases. Experience suggests that while many adults are able to easily visualize the ways of stacking 1, 2, and 3 cubes in columns, younger students are

TABLE 3.5 Number of Ways of Stacking 2 Cubes in Columns

Number of Columns	Number of Ways
1	1
2	1
Total	2

TABLE 3.6 Number of Ways of Stacking One Cube in Column

Number of Columns	Number of Ways
1	1
Total	1

not. Because the data from these first three cases are critical to establishing the patterns underlying the data collected for future cases, it is important that students have an opportunity to see and review how these first three pieces of data are actually obtained.

Predicting the Next Case

At this point in the exploration, tell students you want them to try to predict the total number of different ways 6 cubes can be stacked in columns with at least 1 cube in each column without actually building the arrangements. Solicit predictions from students and write them on the board. You can expect several different responses, but a good number of students are likely to predict the correct number, 32.

Verifying the Prediction

Once the predictions for the number of different ways to stack 6 cubes in columns have been recorded, direct students to find out if the predictions are correct. Suggest that they do so by actually building the arrangements and recording the data obtained in a table. You can distribute an activity sheet (see Activity Sheet 3.3 in Figure 3.26) for students to use, or merely write the information on the blackboard.

Take 6 cubes and show all the different ways you can stack them in one, two, three, four, five, and six columns. Record the number of different ways you found in the space provided in the table below.

Number of Columns	Number of Ways
1	_____
2	_____
3	_____
4	_____
5	_____
6	_____
Total	_____

FIGURE 3.26   ACTIVITY SHEET 3.3: Stacking 6 Cubes in Columns

To construct all the ways of stacking 6 cubes in columns, students will need a total of 160 cubes. Depending on the number of cubes available, you may want students to work in small groups for this part of the exploration. Thus, for example, with six groups of 4 or 5 students a class of 24 to 30 students can do the activity with fewer than 1,000 cubes (960, to be exact).

Figure 3.27 shows the one way of stacking 6 cubes in one column.

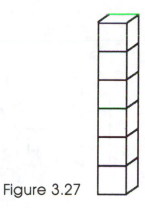

Figure 3.27

Figure 3.28 shows the five different ways of stacking six cubes in two columns.

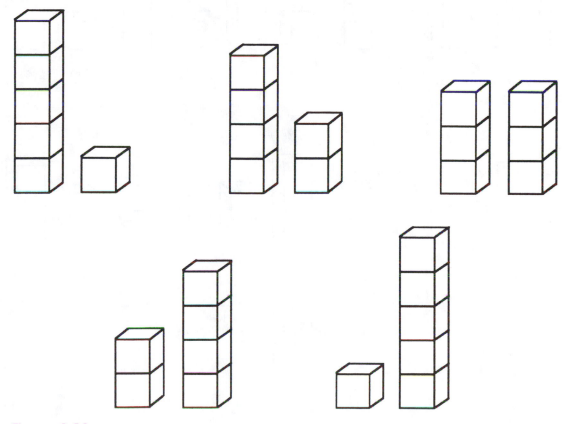

Figure 3.28

Figure 3.29 shows the ten different ways of stacking 6 cubes in three columns.

Figure 3.29

Figure 3.30 shows the ten different ways of stacking 6 cubes in four columns.

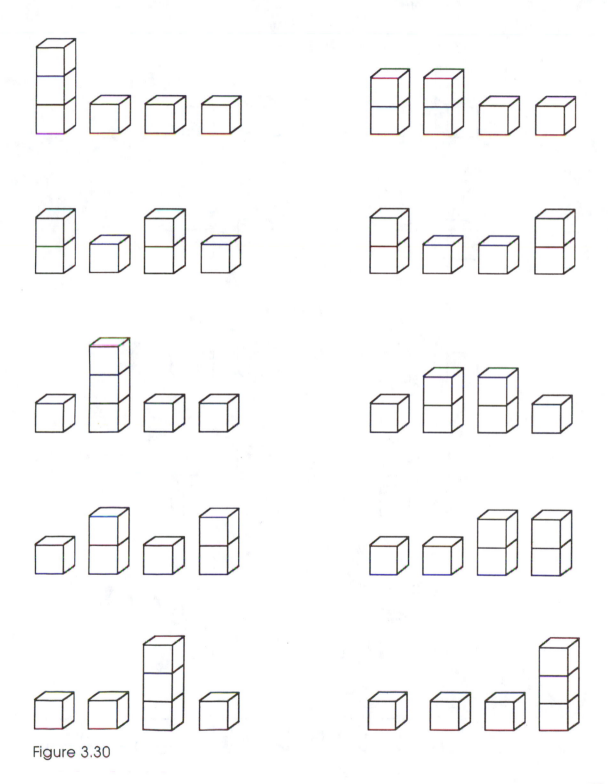

Figure 3.30

Figure 3.31 shows the five different ways of stacking 6 cubes in five columns. Figure 3.32 shows the one way of stacking 6 cubes in six columns.

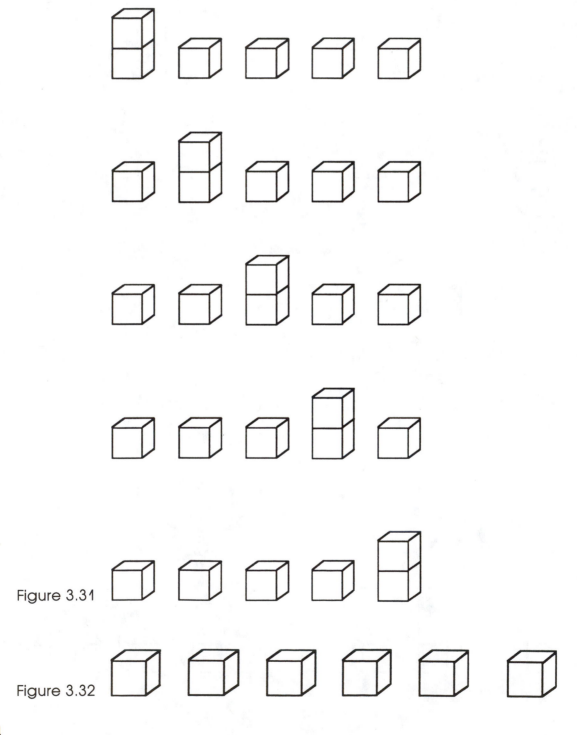

Figure 3.31

Figure 3.32

Table 3.7 summarizes the data on the different ways of stacking 6 cubes.

TABLE 3.7 Number of Ways of Stacking 6 Cubes in Columns

Number of Columns	Number of Ways
1	1
2	5
3	10
4	10
5	5
6	1
Total	32

(i) If the number of cubes available in your classroom is considerably less than 1,000, a good alternative way to explore the activity is to separate the problem into its component pieces and to assign various parts of the problem to different small groups. Thus, one group could be asked to find all of the ways of stacking 6 cubes in three columns, while another group could be asked to find all of the ways of stacking 6 cubes in five columns. Then, after students have had sufficient time to collect the data, you can summarize the results for the class and record them on the blackboard. Doing the activity in this way requires a total of only 160 cubes.

Developing a General Method

To set the stage for this activity, tell students that you are interested in having them develop a method for determining the total number of different ways of stacking any number of cubes, n, in columns. Explain further that you also want them to be able to determine the number of ways of stacking the cubes in a specified number of columns without actually having to construct and count the arrangements.

Begin the activity by asking,

"Who can tell me the minimum number of columns in which the *n* cubes can be stacked?" (*Answer:* All of the cubes can be stacked in one column.)

Then ask,

"What is the maximum number of columns in which the *n* cubes can be stacked?" (*Answer:* If each column contains only 1 cube, the maximum number of columns will be *n*.)

(i) A good way to reinforce these ideas on the minimum and maximum number of columns in which cubes can be stacked is to ask students to state the minimum and maximum number of columns for various amounts of cubes. Thus, you might ask them to tell you the maximum and minimum number of columns for 10 cubes, 13 cubes, and so on. If you do so, it is a good idea actually to place the cubes for all students to see showing the actual number of columns. This helps them visualize the result more easily.

At this point in the activity, ask

"Does anyone know how many different ways there are of stacking 7 cubes in columns?" (*Answer:* The total number of ways is 64.)

Be prepared for many students to say no. A few students will likely respond with 64 as the number of ways to stack the cubes. If you receive such a response, ask the students to explain why they think 64 is the correct number. Usually these students will explain that 64 is the answer because it is double (or twice) 32, the number of ways of stacking 6 cubes in six columns. This response or a similar one is generally based on the students' having observed a pattern in the data collected, organized, and recorded thus far in the tables on the blackboard. As illustrated in Table 3.8, they recognize that each succeeding total for the number of ways to stack cubes in columns is twice the preceding total.

TABLE 3.8 Number of Different Ways to Stack
Cubes in Columns

Number of Cubes	Total Ways to Stack Cubes in Columns
1	1
2	$2 = 2 \times 1$
3	$4 = 2 \times 2$
4	$8 = 2 \times 4$
5	$16 = 2 \times 8$
6	$32 = 2 \times 16$

In most classes a few students may recognize that the total number of ways of stacking n cubes is given by

$$2^{(n-1)}$$

where n is the number of cubes. Thus, for 6 cubes, the total number of ways is

$$2^{(6-1)} = 2^5 = 2 \times 2 \times 2 \times 2 \times 2 = 32.$$

If no student offers this generalization, postpone discussing it until later in the activity.

Whether or not students have suggested 64 as the number of ways of stacking 7 cubes, or the doubling method for determining the total ways of stacking n cubes in n columns, you should proceed with the exploration at this point in the same way, as follows. Distribute Activity Sheet 3.4 to students. It has the information shown in Figure 3.33.

In the following table the entries in row 3 are 1, 2, and 1. These are the number of ways of stacking 3 cubes in one, two, and three columns, respectively.

The information in row 2 is the number of ways of stacking 2 cubes in one and two columns. The information in row 1 is the number of ways of stacking 1 cube in one column.

On the blackboard are data collected in class on the number of ways of stacking 4 cubes in four columns, 5 cubes in five columns, and 6 cubes in six columns. Take those data and reorganize them by completing the table.

Number of Cubes	Total Ways to Stack Cubes in Columns	Ways to Stack Cubes by Number of Columns					
		1	2	3	4	5	6
1	1	1					
2	2	1	1				
3	4	1	2	1			
4	8	—	—	—	—		
5	16	—	—	—	—	—	
6	32	—	—	—	—	—	—

FIGURE 3.33   ACTIVITY SHEET 3.4: Number of Different Ways to Stack Cubes in Columns

The Activity Sheet asks students to take the data previously collected and recorded on the blackboard (for stacking up to 6 cubes) and reorganize them differently in a new table. The reorganized data are presented in Table 3.9. It provides the missing data students are asked to supply in order to complete Activity Sheet 3.4.

TABLE 3.9   Number of Different Ways to Stack Cubes in Columns

Number of Cubes	Total Number of Ways to Stack Cubes in Columns	Number of Columns					
		1	2	3	4	5	6
1	1	1					
2	2	1	1				
3	4	1	2	1			
4	8	1	3	3	1		
5	16	1	4	6	4	1	
6	32	1	5	10	10	5	1

Testing the General Method

After students have completed the table on Activity Sheet 3.4, review the correct information (presented in Table 3.9) and pose the following question to students.

"By examining the data in the table on Activity Sheet 3.4, what patterns do you observe?"

Let the students discuss their observations in small groups of two to four students. After sufficient time has passed, lead a classwide discussion of student answers. Here, focus attention on the different patterns observed and the explanations given by students. You should expect various answers to the question depending on the sophistication of students in mathematics and their skill in discussing mathematical ideas. In general, most classes are able to generate all or most of the observations that follow from an analysis of the data in Table 3.9.

1.   Each succeeding number in column 2, the "Total" column, is the double of the preceding number in the "Total" column.

2. Each number in column 2, the "Total" column, is a power of 2.

3. In the portion of the table representing "Number of Columns," the last entry in each row is 1.

4. In the column representing one column of cubes in the portion of the table representing "Number of Columns," 1 is always the entry.

5. In the column representing two columns of cubes in the portion of the table representing "Number of Columns," succeeding entries increase by 1.

6. If you start in row 2, in the column representing one column of cubes in the portion of the table representing "Number of Columns," and move diagonally down and to the right, succeeding entries increase by 1.

7. In the column representing three columns of cubes in the portion of the table representing "Number of Columns," the difference between the first and second entries is 2 (i.e., $3 - 1 = 2$), the difference between the second and third entries is 3 (i.e., $6 - 3 = 3$), and the difference between the third and fourth entries is 4 (i.e., $10 - 6 = 4$).

8. The entries in the rows of data in the portion of the table representing "Number of Columns" are symmetrical. That is, row 5 reads 1, 4, 6, 4, 1 both from left to right and from right to left. Similarly, the entries in row 4 read 1, 3, 3, 1 from left to right and from right to left.

9. Each entry in the portion of the table representing the "Number of Columns" equals the sum of two numbers in the row above the entry. These numbers are the one immediately above the entry and the one immediately to the left of that number. Thus, as shown in Table 3.10 by the underlined numbers, the 6 in row 5 equals the sum of the 3 and 3 in row 4. And, the 5 in row 6 equals the sum of the 4 and the 1 in row 5.

(i) Once some or all of these observations have been given and explained by members of the class, many students are able on their own to generate the data for additional rows in the table. A good way to end the activity in this section is to ask students the question, "How many different ways can 7 cubes be stacked in columns?" The correct answer provides the data for the seventh row of the table on Activity Sheet 3.4. This information on the number of ways of stacking 7 cubes is given in Table 3.11.

TABLE 3.10   Number of Different Ways to Stack Cubes in Columns

Number of Cubes	Total Number of Ways to Stack Cubes in Columns	Number of Columns					
		1	2	3	4	5	6
1	1	1					
2	2	1	1				
3	4	1	2	1			
4	8	1	3	3	1		
5	16	1	4	6	4	1	
6	32	1	5	10	10	5	1

TABLE 3.11   Number of Different Ways to Stack 7 Cubes in Columns

Number of Cubes	Total Ways to Stack Cubes in Columns	Number of Columns						
		1	2	3	4	5	6	7
1	1	1						
2	2	1	1					
3	4	1	2	1				
4	8	1	3	3	1			
5	16	1	4	6	4	1		
6	32	1	5	10	10	5	1	
7	64	1	6	15	20	15	6	1

(ii) If students are unable to observe and explain the patterns given in this section, you can help them with proper hints, suggestions, and questions. For example, to motivate their discovery of observation 9, you could ask a student to pick two consecutive numbers in a row and find their sum. Doing this a few times with several students usually leads to someone observing that the sum of two consecutive numbers in a row can be found in the row below the row containing the consecutive numbers. And the sum is located directly beneath the second of the two consecutive numbers. This, of course, is just another way of stating observation 9.

Solving the Original Problem

Once you have established the data for the number of different ways to stack 7 cubes in columns, students have sufficient information to generalize the results obtained thus far for the number of different ways to stack any number of cubes in columns. Depending on the backgrounds of the students, you may want them to state the generalization or, preferably, you may want to guide them to do so with an appropriate line of questioning. If you choose the latter approach, here is an illustrative sample of questions to ask. Expected student responses and sample student explanations are also given to provide further insight into how students can be guided to discover and state a conclusion for the exploration.

Teacher: Who can tell me the number of ways of stacking 8 cubes in one column?

Student: One.

Teacher: Why?

Student: Because if there is only one column all of the 8 cubes must be in that column. So, there is only one way of doing this.

Teacher: Who can tell me the number of ways of stacking 9, 10, 20, or 100 cubes in one column?

Student: It is always one.

Teacher: Can you explain why?

Student: No matter how many cubes you have, if there is only one column, then all of the cubes must be in the one column.

Teacher: Who can tell me the total number of ways of stacking 8 cubes?

Student: It is 128.

Teacher: Why do you think 128 is correct?

Student: I doubled 64, the total number of ways of stacking 7 cubes.

Teacher: Who can tell me the number of ways of stacking 8 cubes in three columns?

Student: It is 21.

Teacher: Why do you think 21 is correct?

Student: I added the 6 and 15 in row seven of Table 3.11.

Giving students an opportunity to verbalize their thinking processes is a very valuable exercise. It helps them learn how to communicate mathematical ideas and helps them gain confidence about doing and discussing mathematics.

At this point in the activity, you should direct student attention (if you have not already done so) to the relationship between the number of cubes being stacked, column 1 in each table, and the total number of different ways to stack those cubes in columns, column 2 in each table. Here, you want to focus student attention first on the fact that each of the numbers representing total ways to stack cubes in columns can be expressed as powers of 2. An effective way of doing so is to develop on the blackboard the information given in Table 3.12.

TABLE 3.12   Multiples of 2 Pattern

Number of Cubes	Total Ways to Stack Cubes in Columns
1	1
2	2
3	$4 = 2 \times 2$
4	$8 = 2 \times 2 \times 2$
5	$16 = 2 \times 2 \times 2 \times 2$
6	$32 = 2 \times 2 \times 2 \times 2 \times 2$
7	$64 = 2 \times 2 \times 2 \times 2 \times 2 \times 2$
8	$128 = 2 \times 2 \times 2 \times 2 \times 2 \times 2 \times 2$

Next, direct student attention to a specific entry in Table 3.12, say the entry for 5 cubes. Point out that

$$2 \times 2 \times 2 \times 2 = 2^4.$$

Similarly,

$$2 \times 2 \times 2 = 2^3, 2 \times 2 = 2^2, \text{ and so on.}$$

Then, add a column to Table 3.12 labeled, "Powers of 2," and record the proper expressions as shown in Table 3.13.

TABLE 3.13   Power of 2 Pattern

Number of Cubes	Total Ways to Stack Cubes in Columns	Power of 2
1	1	
2	2	
3	$4 = 2 \times 2$	2^2
4	$8 = 2 \times 2 \times 2$	2^3
5	$16 = 2 \times 2 \times 2 \times 2$	2^4
6	$32 = 2 \times 2 \times 2 \times 2 \times 2$	2^5
7	$64 = 2 \times 2 \times 2 \times 2 \times 2 \times 2$	2^6
8	$128 = 2 \times 2 \times 2 \times 2 \times 2 \times 2 \times 2$	2^7

Next, ask students the following sequence of questions. Let various students provide answers and explanations. Some responses you might expect are given.

Teacher: Who can tell me the number of ways 9 cubes can be stacked in columns?

Student: The number of ways is 256.

Teacher: What would the correct entry be in the "Powers of 2" column?

Student: Twenty-eight.

Teacher: What would the entry be in the "Powers of 2" column for 10 cubes?

Student: Twenty nine.

Teacher: What would the entry be in the "Powers of Two" column for 11 cubes?

Student: Two hundred ten.

Teacher: Why are the entries for 10 cubes and 11 cubes 29 and 210?

Student: The number is always a power of 2, and the exponent is one less than the number of cubes.

Teacher: What would the entries in the "Power of Two" column be for 20 cubes? . . . for 35 cubes?

Student: Two hundred nineteen, since the power of 2 is one less than 20, and 234, since the power of 2 is one less than 35.

Teacher: If you had n cubes, what would the entry be in the "Powers of 2" column?

Student: $2^{(n-1)}$.

Before continuing, it is useful for you to summarize for students the conclusion just developed in this part of the exploration. Specifically, review for students that the total number of different ways of stacking n cubes in columns is given by the formula

$$Y = 2^{(n-1)}$$

where Y is the total number of ways of stacking the cubes and n is the number of cubes being stacked.

Once the formula $Y = 2^{(n-1)}$ has been stated, show students that the number of different ways to stack 10 cubes in columns is given by

$$Y = 2^{(10-1)} = 2^9 = 512.$$

Introducing Pascal's Triangle

At this point in the development of the stacking cubes problem I like to review the information obtained thus far by directing students to consider the data in Table 3.14. Then, I ask the following questions:

"Does the information in the table look familiar? . . . Do the table data remind you of a topic you may have studied before?"

TABLE 3.14   Number of Different Ways to Stack Cubes in Columns

Number of Cubes	Total Ways to Stack Cubes in Columns	Number of Columns									
		1	2	3	4	5	6	7	8	9	10
1	1	1									
2	2	1	1								
3	4	1	2	1							
4	8	1	4	4	1						
5	16	1	4	6	4	1					
6	32	1	5	10	10	5	1				
7	64	1	6	15	20	15	6	1			
8	128	1	7	21	35	35	21	7	1		
9	256	1	8	28	56	70	56	28	8	1	
10	512	1	9	36	84	126	126	84	36	9	1

In asking these questions, I am giving students an opportunity to recall previously studied material in the event that they may have already explored Pascal's triangle. If they have not, I use this opportunity to introduce and discuss Pascal's triangle and the many interesting features associated with the triangle.

Generally, I first present Pascal's triangle visually, as shown in Table 3.15. Then I invite students to look for and report some of the patterns they observe. Some of the more obvious patterns usually mentioned by students include:

1. Each row of the triangle begins and ends with 1.

2. Diagonals of the triangle form sequence patterns as follows:
    a. One diagonal has entries that are all 1's (see the underlined numbers in Table 3.16).

TABLE 3.15   Pascal's Triangle

```
                        1
                     1     1
                  1     2     1
               1     3     3     1
            1     4     6     4     1
         1     5    10    10     5     1
      1     6    15    20    15     6     1
   1     7    21    35    35    21     7     1
1     8    28    56    70    56    28     8     1
1  9  36  84  126  126  84  36  9  1
```

TABLE 3.16   Pascal's Triangle

```
                        1
                     1     1
                  1     2     1
               1     3     3     1
            1     4     6     4     1
         1     5    10    10     5     1
      1     6    15    20    15     6     1
   1     7    21    35    35    21     7     1
1     8    28    56    70    56    28     8     1
1  9  36  84  126  126  84  36  9  1
```

b. One diagonal has entries that increase by 1 (see the underlined numbers in Table 3.17).

c. One diagonal has entries that differ by consecutive integers starting with 2 (see the underlined numbers in Table 3.18).

TABLE 3.17   Pascal's Triangle

```
                          1
                       1     1
                    1     2     1
                 1     3     3     1
              1     4     6     4     1
           1     5    10    10     5     1
        1     6    15    20    15     6     1
     1     7    21    35    35    21     7     1
  1     8    28    56    70    56    28     8     1
1     9    36    84   126   126    84    36     9     1
```

TABLE 3.18   Pascal's Triangle

```
                          1
                       1     1
                    1     2     1
                 1     3     3     1
              1     4     6     4     1
           1     5    10    10     5     1
        1     6    15    20    15     6     1
     1     7    21    35    35    21     7     1
  1     8    28    56    70    56    28     8     1
1     9    36    84   126   126    84    36     9     1
```

3. The sum of each row is a power of 2. Thus, for example, row 4 is $1 + 3 + 3 + 1 = 8 = 2^3$.

4. Each entry in the body of the triangle is the sum of the two numbers directly above it in the triangle. Thus, 20 in row 7 equals the $10 + 10$ in row 6.

Often, after the foregoing observations have been discussed, students recognize that the entries in Pascal's triangle are identical to the entries in Table 3.14. The only difference is that the entries in Table 3.14 are oriented to look something like a right triangle, whereas the entries in Pascal's triangle are oriented to look something like an equilateral triangle.

I conclude this activity with the observation that Pascal's triangle can be useful in solving the stacking cubes problem previously explored. The entries in each row of Pascal's triangle provide the data for the number of different ways a specified number of cubes can be stacked in columns. Thus, row 4 of Pascal's triangle is 1, 3, 3, 1 and $1 + 3 + 3 + 1 = 8$. The number 8 is the total number of different ways 4 cubes can be stacked in one, two, three, and four columns. Further, the entries in row 4 (i.e., 1, 3, 3, 1) correspond to the number of different ways to stack 4 cubes in one column (i.e., one way), to stack 4 cubes in two columns (i.e., three ways), to stack 4 cubes in three columns (i.e., three ways), and to stack 4 cubes in four columns (i.e., one way).

Section F   Extensions

Generating the Triangular Numbers

After the stacking cubes in columns problem has been explored and Pascal's triangle discussed, I like to broaden students' mathematical problem-solving experience by introducing the triangular numbers and developing a formula to generate them. A brief outline of my method follows. It also provides an opportunity for students to see how previously learned ideas in mathematics can be helpful in solving new problems.

I quickly review with students the following generalizations associated with the stacking cubes in columns problem.

1. The number of ways of stacking n cubes in one (or n) columns is always one.

2. The number of ways of stacking n cubes in 2 (or $n - 1$) columns is $n - 1$.

Then, I ask students how we might develop a formula for determining the number of different ways to stack n cubes in three columns. Usually, some students recognize from the previous work with the stacking cubes in columns problem that for $n > 3$, as the number of cubes increases by 1, the number of ways to stack the cubes in three columns increases according to the pattern shown in Table 3.19.

TABLE 3.19   Pattern

Number of Cubes, n	Ways to Stack Cubes in Three Columns	
3	1	
	)2	
4	3	)1
	)3	
5	6	)1
	)4	
6	10	)1
	)5	
7	15	

Notice in the table the well-known sequence:

$$1, 3, 6, 10, 15, \ldots$$

It represents the first five triangular numbers pictured in Figure 3.34. The triangular numbers are given by the formula

Figure 3.34

$$Y = \tfrac{1}{2}a(a + 1),$$

where a is the number of rows of dots in the triangle. Thus, for the sixth triangular number shown in Figure 3.35, there are six rows of dots. Therefore, the triangular number represented in Figure 3.35 is

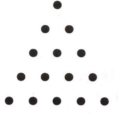

Figure 3.35

$$\tfrac{1}{2}a(a + 1) = \tfrac{1}{2}(6)\,(7) = 21.$$

There are many ways to develop the formula for the triangular numbers. One interesting approach for students is based on the manner in which the triangular numbers are constructed using dots. Glance at the sixth triangular number shown in Figure 3.35. Notice that there are six rows and that each row contains one more dot than the preceding row. Thus, for the sixth triangular number in Figure 3.35, there are six rows with

$$1 + 2 + 3 + 4 + 5 + 6 = 21$$

dots in all. Therefore, the triangular number 21 is the sum of the consecutive integers from 1 to 6.

In general the ath triangular number is given by the sum of the positive consecutive integers from 1 to a. In other words, the ath triangular number equals

$$1 + 2 + 3 + \ldots + (a - 2) + (a - 1) + a.$$

The sum of the integers from 1 to a can be found as follows:

1. Write

$$1 + 2 + 3 + \ldots + (a - 2) + (a - 1) + a \qquad \text{(A)}$$

2. Reverse (A):

$$a + (a - 1) + (a - 2) + \ldots + 3 + 2 + 1 \qquad \text{(B)}$$

3. Add (A) and (B) to form their sum:

$$1 + 2 + 3 + \ldots + (a - 2) + (a - 1) + a \qquad \text{(A)}$$
$$a + (a - 1) + (a - 2) + \ldots + 3 + 2 + 1 \qquad \text{(B)}$$
$$\overline{(a + 1) + (a + 1) + (a + 1) + \ldots + (a + 1) + (a + 1) + (a + 1)}$$

4. Notice that the sum is twice the sum of the integers from 1 to a.

5. Also, in the sum there are a terms of $(a + 1)$.

6. Thus, $a(a + 1)$ is twice the sum of the integers from 1 to a.

7. Therefore, $\frac{1}{2}a(a + 1)$ is the sum of the integers from 1 to a.

Once the formula above is derived, demonstrate to students how it can be used to obtain the triangular numbers by showing that

$$\frac{1}{2}a(a + 1)$$

the sixth triangular number is

$$1 + 2 + \ldots + 5 + 6$$

and equals

$$\tfrac{1}{2}(6)\,(6 + 1) = \tfrac{1}{2}(6)\,(7) = \tfrac{1}{2}(42) = 21.$$

I like to conclude this extension activity with older students by showing that applying this formula,

$$\tfrac{1}{2}a(a + 1),$$

to the problem of determining the number of ways of stacking a cubes in three columns requires one modification. With 1 and 2 cubes you can not create three columns. Hence, the first time you can use the formula is when a, the number of cubes, is 3. But when a is 3,

$$\tfrac{1}{2}a(a + 1) = \tfrac{1}{2}(3)\,(3 + 1) = \tfrac{1}{2}(12) = 6,$$

and 6 is the third triangular number, not the first triangular number, 1.

By substituting $a - 2$ for a in

$$\tfrac{1}{2}a(a + 1),$$

you can obtain a formula that gives the correct result for $a = 3$. Thus,

$$\tfrac{1}{2}(a - 2)(a - 2 + 1) = \tfrac{1}{2}(a - 2)(a - 1)$$

Notice that when $a = 3$,

$$\tfrac{1}{2}(a - 2)(a - 1) = \tfrac{1}{2}(3 - 2)(3 - 1) = \tfrac{1}{2}(1)(2) = 1$$

and when $a = 6$,

$$\tfrac{1}{2}(6 - 2)(6 - 1) = \tfrac{1}{2}(4)(5) = 10.$$

These results, 1 when $a = 3$ and 10 when $a = 6$, correspond to the number of ways of stacking 3 cubes and 6 cubes, respectively, in three columns.

Sums of Numbers in Pascal's Triangle

1. What is the sum of all the numbers in the first three rows of Pascal's Triangle?

2. What is the sum of all the numbers in the first 10 rows of Pascal's triangle?

3. What is the sum of all the numbers in the first n rows of Pascal's triangle?

Exploring Alternative Definitions

In the stacking cubes in columns exploration, there were eight different ways to stack four cubes in one, two, three, and four columns as shown in Figures 3.16, 3.17, 3.18, and 3.19. Following are two alternative definitions for the phrase "different ways." For each of these definitions, how many different ways can 4 cubes be stacked columns?

1. If one arrangement of cubes can be rotated to form another arrangement of the cubes, these two arrangements will be considered the same, not different.

2. Label the 4 cubes A, B, C, and D. Consider the arrangement of cubes in a stack (e.g., ABCD) to be different if the labeled cubes are in a different order—for example, ACBD.

ACTIVITY SHEET 3.1

Stacking 4 Cubes in Columns

Take 4 cubes and show all the different ways you can stack them in one, two, three, and four columns. Record the number of different ways you found in the space provided in the table below.

Number of Columns	Number of Ways
1	____
2	____
3	____
4	____
Total	____

ACTIVITY SHEET 3.2

Stacking 5 Cubes in Columns

Take 5 cubes and show all the different ways you can stack them in one, two, three, four, and five columns. Record the number of ways you found in the space provided in the table below.

Number of Columns	*Number of Ways*
1	____
2	____
3	____
4	____
5	____
Total	____

A C T I V I T Y   S H E E T   3 . 3

Stacking 6 Cubes in Columns

Take 6 cubes and show all the different ways you can stack them in one, two, three, four, five, and six columns. Record the number of different ways you found in the space provided in the table below.

Number of Columns	*Number of Ways*
1	____
2	____
3	____
4	____
5	____
6	____
Total	____

ACTIVITY SHEET 3.4

Number of Different Ways to Stack Cubes in Columns

In the following table the entries in row 3 are 1, 2, and 1. These are the number of ways of stacking 3 cubes in one, two, and three columns, respectively.

The information in row 2 is the number of ways of stacking 2 cubes in one and two columns. The information in row 1 is the number of ways of stacking 1 cube in 1 column.

On the blackboard are data collected in class on the number of ways of stacking 4 cubes in four columns, 5 cubes in five columns, and 6 cubes in six columns. Take those data and reorganize them by completing the table.

Number of Cubes	Total Ways to Stack Cubes in Columns	Ways to Stack Cubes by Number of Columns					
		1	2	3	4	5	6
1	1	1					
2	2	1	1				
3	4	1	2	1			
4	8	—	—	—	—		
5	16	—	—	—	—	—	
6	32	—	—	—	—	—	—

DISCOVERING
an Application
for the Formula
$Y = 2^{(n-1)}$
with Cuisenaire Rods

CHAPTER CONTENTS

Section A   The Problem

Section B   Unit Objectives

Primary Objectives for This Exploration

Secondary Objectives for This Exploration

Section C   Materials Required

Section D   Description of the Cuisenaire Rods

Section E   Sequence of Activities

Introducing Rod Trains
Understanding the Problem
Collecting Data
Making a Prediction
Checking the Prediction
Forming a Hypothesis
Verifying the Hypothesis
Organizing the Data
Analyzing the Data
Solving the Problem
Generalizing the Result

Section F   Extensions

Introducing or Reviewing Pascal's Triangle
Finding Trains for an O + R Train
Motivating $Y = 2^{(n-1)} - 1$
Exploring Another Definition of Equivalent Trains

Activity Sheet

Section A The Problem

Using Cuisenaire rods, how many rod trains can be formed equivalent in length to an orange rod?

Section B Unit Objectives

Primary Objectives for this Exploration

1. Experiencing the problem-solving steps: (1) understanding a problem, (2) devising a solution plan, (3) experimenting to collect data, (4) making and checking predictions from previous data, (5) forming and verifying a hypothesis, (6) organizing data systematically, (7) analyzing data, and (8) stating a conclusion.

2. Developing the meaning of the word *different* in the question, "How many different trains are there equivalent in length to an orange rod?"

3. Developing the formula, $Y = 2^{(n-1)}$, through a sequence of activities as the solution of a specific problem motivated by the use of Cuisenaire rods.

4. Introducing Pascal's triangle.

Secondary Objectives for This Exploration

1. Clarifying the importance of order when arranging objects.

2. Defining the concept of a function.

3. Explaining the meaning of an algorithm.

4. Defining the meaning of symmetry.

5. Exploring the properties of square numbers.

Section C   Materials Required

1 set of Cuisenaire rods for each student

1 activity sheet for each student (a reproducible copy of the activity sheet is provided at the end of this chapter)

Section D   Description of the Cuisenaire Rods

Cuisenaire rods are a set of rectangular prisms of different lengths, as shown in Figure 4.1. The rods measure 1 cm × 1 cm × n cm, where n is a whole number from one 1 to 10 representing the length of the rod in centimeters. The set of Cuisenaire rods has 10 distinct lengths, each of which is a different color, as shown in Table 4.1.

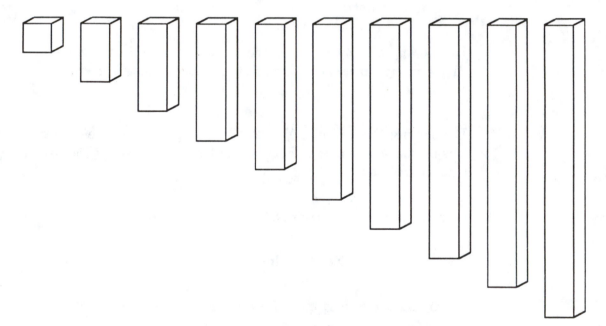

Figure 4.1

When referring to specific Cuisenaire rods, it is customary to name them with a single letter, as shown in Table 4.2. Notice that the White, Red, Green, Purple, Yellow, Dark Green, and Orange rods are named W, R, G, P, Y, D, and O, respectively, using the first letter in the name of the color. Because the colors Black, Brown, and Blue all begin with the same letter, B, rods of those

TABLE 4.1   Colors of Cuisenaire Rods

Dimension of Cuisenaire Rod (cm)	Color of the Rod
$1 \times 1 \times 1$	White
$1 \times 1 \times 2$	Red
$1 \times 1 \times 3$	Green
$1 \times 1 \times 4$	Purple
$1 \times 1 \times 5$	Yellow
$1 \times 1 \times 6$	Dark Green
$1 \times 1 \times 7$	Black
$1 \times 1 \times 8$	Brown
$1 \times 1 \times 9$	Blue
$1 \times 1 \times 10$	Orange

TABLE 4.2   Single-Letter Names of Cuisenaire Rods

Dimension of Cuisenaire Rod (cm)	Color of the Rod	Single-Letter Name of the Rod
$1 \times 1 \times 1$	White	W
$1 \times 1 \times 2$	Red	R
$1 \times 1 \times 3$	Green	G
$1 \times 1 \times 4$	Purple	P
$1 \times 1 \times 5$	Yellow	Y
$1 \times 1 \times 6$	Dark Green	D
$1 \times 1 \times 7$	Black	K
$1 \times 1 \times 8$	Brown	N
$1 \times 1 \times 9$	Blue	E
$1 \times 1 \times 10$	Orange	O

colors are referred to by the letters K, N, and E, respectively, using the last letter in the name of the color. Figure 4.2 shows the 10 Cuisenaire rods with their single-letter names.

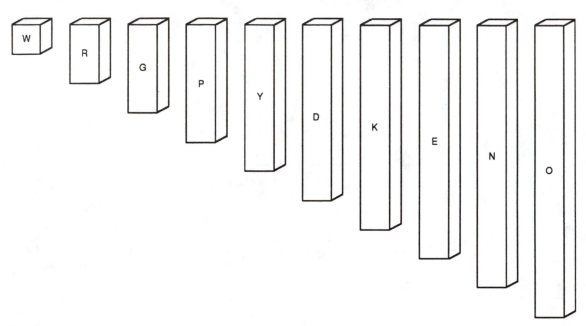

Figure 4.2

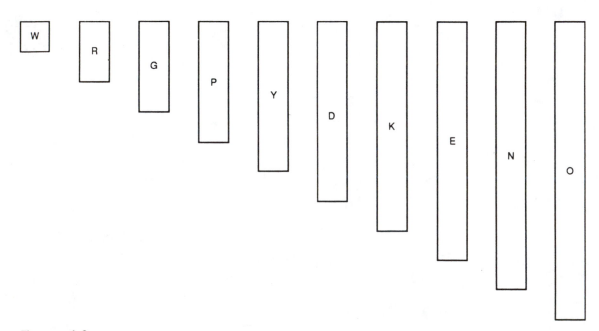

Figure 4.3

Because Cuisenaire rods are three-dimensional objects, the figures accompanying the text are drawn in three dimensions. In actual classroom settings, you will find it much easier to draw rod figures in two dimensions, unless you are very good at drawing three-dimensional shapes. Thus, you can draw the various rods as shown in Figure 4.3 or even quickly sketch them freehand as shown in Figure 4.4.

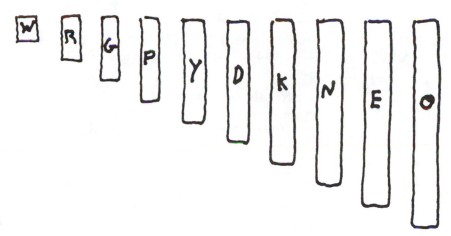

Figure 4.4

Section E   The Sequence of Activities

Introducing Rod Trains

Show students a light green rod and ask,

> "How many white rods does it take to make a light green rod?"

Then say,

> "Show me how many white rods make a light green rod by placing the white rods end to end."

Most students will place the rods correctly, as shown in Figure 4.5. Reinforce the idea that 3 white rods are equivalent in length to 1 light green rod by placing the rods as shown in Figure 4.6. Tell students,

> "The 3 white rods form a three-car train while the light green rod forms a one-car train."

Figure 4.5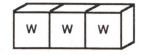

Next, tell students,

> "Place a yellow rod on the table."

Figure 4.6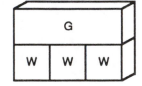

Then say,

> "Make a two-car train that is the same length as the yellow rod."

You should expect varied responses, as there are 4 possible two-car trains that students might form:

P,W
G,R
R,G
W,P

The 4 two-car trains are shown in Figure 4.7.

(i) In this chapter, all rod trains will be written as a string of letters separated by commas. The letters used will be those designated to identify the various individual rods—W for the white rod, R for the red rod, G for the light green rod, P for the purple rod, Y for the yellow rod, D for the dark green rod,

K for the black rod, N for the brown rod, E for the blue rod, and O for the orange rod. Thus, a train identified as W,R,G would be the three-car train formed by placing a white rod, a red rod, and a green rod end to end in that order.

Circulate around the room to ensure that each student makes a correct two-car train. If students are having trouble making correct two-car trains, help them one on one before proceeding.
Next, tell students,

"Make all the different three-car trains that are the same length as a yellow rod."

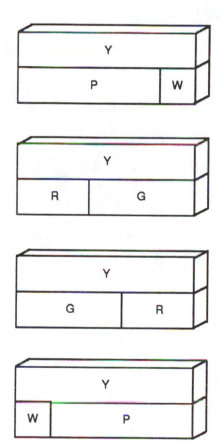

Figure 4.7

Again, you should expect varied answers. Some students will show 2 three-car trains,

G,W,W
R,R,W

as pictured in Figure 4.8 (*Note:* In Figure 4.8 and Figure 4.9, the one-car yellow rod is shown above the trains depicted to provide quick visual confirmation that the trains are equivalent in length to the yellow rod.)

Other students will show the 6 trains,

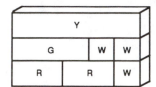

Figure 4.8

G,W,W
R,R,W
R,W,R
W,G,W
W,R,R
W,W,G

as pictured in Figure 4.9.

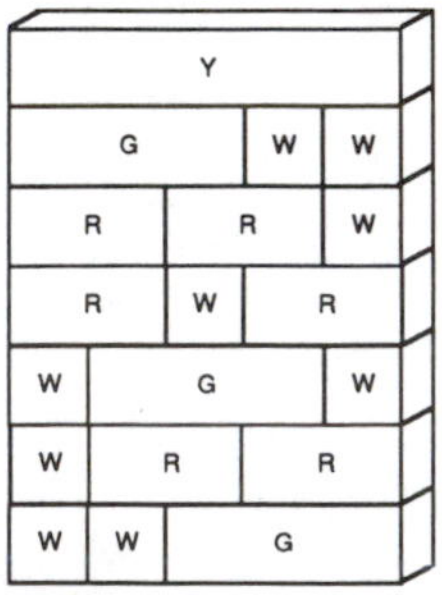

Figure 4.9

Students who show the 6 three-car trains in Figure 4.9 generally consider different arrangements of the rods by color as forming different trains. To illustrate this interpretation, consider using 1 white rod and 2 red rods to form different three-car trains. The white rod can be the first car, in which case the train will be

W,R,R,

or the white rod can be the second car, in which case the train will be

$$R,W,R,$$

or the white rod can be the third car, in which case the train will be

$$R,R,W.$$

These 3 three-car trains, the

$$W,R,R$$
$$R,W,R$$
$$R,R,W$$

are shown in Figure 4.10. They are the only three-car trains that can be formed if the arrangements of the 1 white and 2 red rods are to be unique.

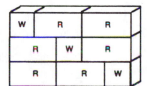

Figure 4.10

For another example illustrating the arrangement of rods by color interpretation, consider 1 green rod and 2 white rods. Together, these rods will form 3 different three-car trains,

$$W,W,G$$
$$W,G,W$$
$$G,W,W$$

as shown in Figure 4.11

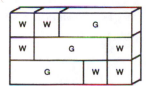

Figure 4.11

Students who show the 2 three-car trains in Figure 4.8 in response to the instruction,

"Make all three-car trains the same length as a yellow rod,"

generally are not considering different arrangements of rods by color as forming different trains. Instead, they interpret trains as being different only if the set of rods used to form the trains is different. Thus, they consider each of the 3 three-car trains in Figure 4.10 as being a single train rather than three different trains because each of the trains is formed from the same set of 3 rods, 1 white rod and 2 red rods.

(ii) Some students will show 4 or 5 three-car trains for this activity. Often, these students are using the interpretation for the problem that would lead to the six-train solution, but they may not build the trains in any systematic way and thus fail to find all of them. In some cases, the students merely form the trains on a random, trial-and-error basis and give little or no thought as to what it means to "make" a three-car train or how the task should be accomplished. This, of course, presents an ideal opportunity to discuss with students the importance in problem solving of (1) understanding the problem before you attempt to solve it, and (2) devising a plan for how you initially intend to approach the solution of the problem.

(iii) Some advanced students may state that there are 12 different three-car trains the same length as the yellow rod. These students generally think about the problem as follows. They take the set of 1 white and 2 red rods. Since there are 2 red rods, they might call one of them R1 and the other R2. If the white rod is the first car, then the second car can be either R1 or R2. This leads to two trains in which the white rod is the first car,

W,R1,R2
W,R2,R3

Similarly, if the white rod is the second or third car, in each case there will be 2 more trains as follows:

R1,W,R2
R2,W,R1

R1,R2,W
R2,R1,W

This yields a total of 6 three-car trains equivalent in length to the yellow rod using 1 white rod and 2 red rods. A similar line of reasoning yields a total of 6 three-car trains equivalent in length to the yellow rod using 1 green rod and 2 white rods.

Thus, there are 12 three-car trains in all using this particular interpretation.

At this point in the activity, explain to students that any of the interpretations for determining which trains are different might make sense given a particular context in which the phrase is used. Tell them that for the train activities in this chapter you will be using the interpretation that different arrangements of rods by color will form different trains. Thus, for the yellow rod, as shown in Figure 4.9, in this activity there are 6 different three-car trains the same length as the yellow rod. They are:

$$G,W,W \quad R,W,R \quad W,R,R$$
$$R,R,W \quad W,G,W \quad W,W,G$$

You can check student understanding of this interpretation by asking them to form all 10 of the different three-car trains that are the same length as a dark green rod. The 10 trains are:

$$P,W,W \quad G,W,R \quad R,R,R$$
$$W,P,W \quad G,R,W$$
$$W,W,P \quad W,G,R$$
$$\qquad\qquad W,R,G$$
$$\qquad\qquad R,W,G$$
$$\qquad\qquad R,G,W$$

Figure 4.12 shows the 10 three-car trains that are the same length as a dark green rod.

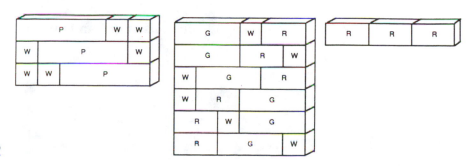

Figure 4.12

Understanding the Problem

Once most students understand how to form all the different rod trains equivalent in length to a given rod, pose the following problem:

> "How many different trains are there equivalent in length to an orange rod?"

Explain to students that you are going to have them solve this problem through a series of activities. Tell them that by piecing together the answers to a number of related problems, they will be able to determine the answer to the question. Then, as the first activity, give them this instruction,

> "Build all the trains equivalent in length to a purple rod."

> *(i) It is a good idea to let students work cooperatively on this problem in groups of about four students. Their interaction as they attempt to do the problem enhances the learning and problem-solving experiences in the exploration.*

After providing sufficient time for students to work, ask how many trains they have discovered that are the same length as the purple rod. Be prepared for a variety of answers, as not all the students will fully understand yet how to form all the equivalent-length trains. During this phase of the activity, seek consensus among the students and record the correct number of trains on the blackboard as you collect data from students. Actually sketch the trains on the blackboard. Take care to sketch the trains in a somewhat random fashion by asking individual students to suggest a train until all 8 have been obtained. If students do not generate all 8 of the trains, you can add any that are missing or you can motivate students to find them by saying something along the lines of

> "There are 2 trains missing. Can you find them?"

Figure 4.13 shows the 8 trains that are the same length as the purple rod.

(ii) You will find drawing rod trains in two dimensions much easier and quicker than trying to draw them in three dimensions. And because you will be drawing these trains on the blackboard during actual instructional time, ease and speed of creating the figures are important factors. You will want to maximize interaction time with students while minimizing the amount of time necessary for creating the figures. Therefore, I recommend that when you are recording the rod trains on the blackboard you actually sketch the trains freehand in two dimensions as rectangles, rather than in three dimensions as rectangular prisms. Such sketches are presented in Figure 4.14. Your freehand sketches of trains at the blackboard will not look as much like rectangles as the figures drawn in this chapter.

Complete this phase of the activity by reviewing for students that there are 8 trains equivalent in length to a purple rod. Point out that the purple rod itself is included as a one-car train. Carefully write the number 8 above the trains sketched on the blackboard, as shown in Figure 4.15.

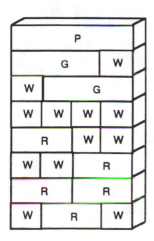

Figure 4.13

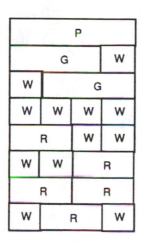

Figure 4.14

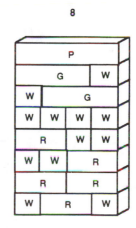

Figure 4.15

Then ask students,

"How many of the 8 trains equivalent in length to a purple rod have 3 cars?"

As students identify a particular three-car train (e.g., the R,W,W train) point to the train sketched on the blackboard and record the number 3 to the right of the train. This indicates that the train has 3 cars, as shown in Figure 4.16.

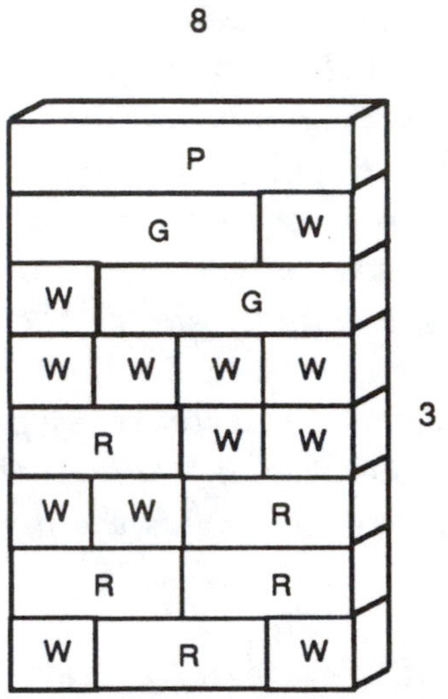

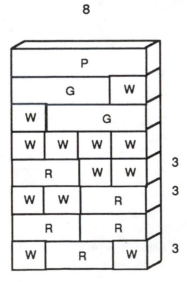

Figure 4.16

When all 3 of the three-car trains have been identified, as shown in Figure 4.17, ask students,

"How many cars will the train with the fewest cars have?" (*Answer:* The train with the fewest cars has 1 car; it is the purple rod itself.)

Figure 4.17

Then write 1 on the blackboard next to the one-car train, as shown in Figure 4.18.

Next, ask,

"How many cars will the train with the most cars have?" (*Answer:* The train with the most cars has 4 cars; it is the train with 4 white rods.)

Write 4 next to the 1 four-car train on the blackboard, as shown in Figure 4.19.

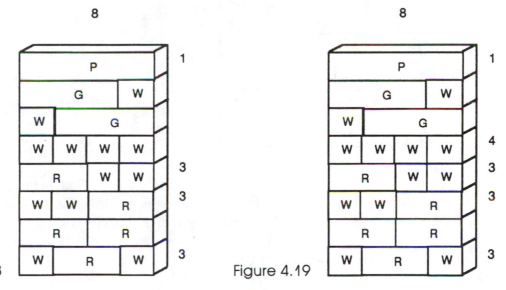

Figure 4.18

Figure 4.19

Finally, ask,

"How many trains will have 2 cars?" (*Answer:* There will be 3 two-car trains, the G,W train, the W,G train, and the R,R train.)

Then write 2 next to these two-car trains as shown in Figure 4.20.

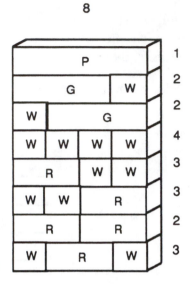

Figure 4.20

Once the information in Figure 4.20 has been collected, explained, and recorded, review quickly with students that the purple rod has 8 different equivalent-length trains, and that one of them has 1 car, 3 of them have 2 cars, 3 of them have 3 cars and 1 of them has 4 cars. Point out that

$$1 + 3 + 3 + 1 = 8,$$

the total number of equivalent-length trains.

(iii) It is not obvious to students that, when building trains equivalent in length to a particular rod, the train with the fewest cars always has 1 car. Nor is it obvious that the train with the most cars always has the number of cars corresponding to the number of white rods in the train formed by all white rods. Thus, a good side trip at this point, if time permits, is to develop these ideas by asking students to build the trains with the fewest and most cars for various rods. It is important to allow one or more students to verbalize the generalization in their own words, as the ability to do so is a valuable skill in learning and understanding mathematics. You can guide them into recognizing and verbalizing the generalization, if necessary, by asking, "If I give you a rod, how can you always tell the number of cars in the train with the fewest cars? . . . in the train with the most cars?"

Now, tell students that the next series of activities will help them explore and answer the original problem posed: finding the number of trains that can be formed that are equivalent in length to an orange rod.

Collecting Data

Instruct each student to form all the trains equivalent in length to a green rod. While students are working, move around the class and help one on one any students who are having difficulty finding the different trains. At this point, however, most students will have no difficulty forming the trains.

Provide sufficient time for student exploration. Then ask various students to name specific trains while you sketch them on the blackboard. Do so to the left of the trains already sketched on the blackboard that are equivalent in length to the purple rod so that the information will appear as shown in Figure 4.21. When you finish sketching all the 4 trains that are the same length as the green rod, write the number 4 above the trains as shown in Figure 4.22 and indicate the number of one-car, two-car, and three-car trains as also shown.

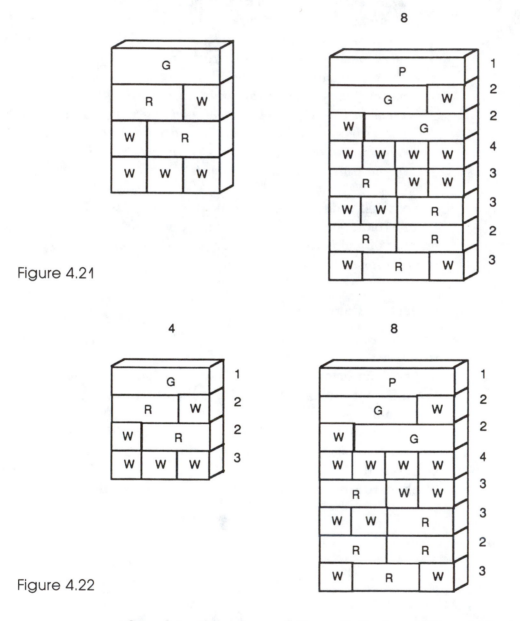

Figure 4.21

Figure 4.22

Complete this phase of the activity by asking students how many trains can be formed that are equivalent in length to a red rod and how many trains can be formed that are equivalent in length to a white rod. Sketch the trains (to the left of those for the green and purple rods already sketched on the blackboard) so that the information on the blackboard appears as shown in Figure 4.23.

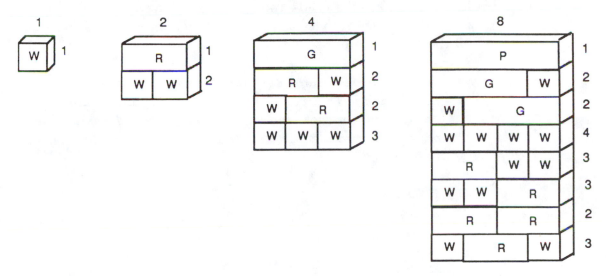

Figure 4.23

(i) Arranging the placement of your sketches on the blackboard as shown in Figure 4.23 is important. Doing so sets the stage for students to recognize visually the developing patterns and relationships important in solving the remaining problems and activities in this chapter.

Making a Prediction

Next ask students to predict, without actually forming the trains, how many trains they think are equivalent in length to a yellow rod. Generally, some students will reply with the number 16. Ask them to explain how they arrived at this answer. Usually they will say their prediction is based on doubling the number of trains for the purple rod. If no prediction is forthcoming, proceed to the next activity anyway.

Checking the Prediction

Tell students to check whether or not the prediction is correct by actually building all the trains that can be formed that are equivalent in length to the yellow rod. If a prediction was not obtained, merely treat this activity as an opportunity for students to form all the trains in order to obtain the result.

(i) It is a good idea to have students work in small groups on this activity. This is particularly true if you do not have enough rods for each student. To form all 16 of the trains that are equivalent in length to a yellow rod requires a total of 48 rods, as follows:

1 Yellow
2 Purple
5 Green
12 Red
28 White

Thus, if you have students work separately, each one will need a complete set of rods since the standard student set contains a total of 72 rods. By placing students in small groups, you can have them do this activity with a limited number of rod sets. By forming groups of 4, you could handle a class of 28 students with just 7 Cuisenaire rod sets.

Provide ample time for student work and then, as before, ask specific students to tell you the trains they have discovered. As students describe the trains they obtained, sketch the trains on the blackboard, this time to the right of the trains already on the blackboard for the purple rod. Continue sketching the trains until all 16 trains have been recorded. As before, indicate the number of cars in each train by writing the appropriate number to the right of each individual train. Also, record the total number of trains above the one-car yellow rod. Figure 4.24 shows all 16 of the trains and identifies the total number of trains and the number of cars in each train.

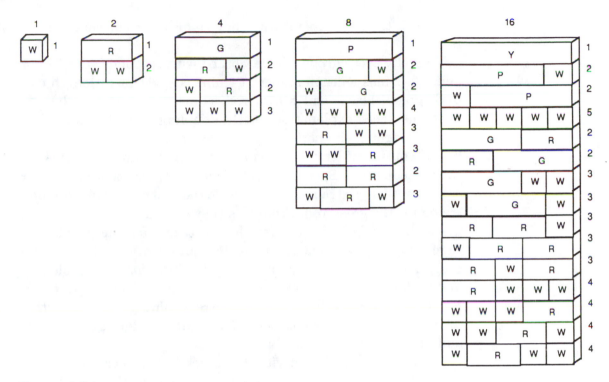

Figure 4.24

Forming a Hypothesis

Review quickly the number of trains that can be formed equivalent in length to each of the rods explored so far—the white, red, green, purple, and yellow rods. Do so by referring to the information already collected and recorded on the blackboard (see Figure 4.24). Then ask students to make a prediction, without actually building the trains,

> "How many trains do you think can be formed equivalent in length to the dark green, black, and brown rods?" (*Answer:* The number of equivalent-length trains is 32, 64, and 128, respectively.)

Also, ask them to explain why they think their answers are correct.

Virtually every group I have worked with responds with 32, 64, and 128 trains as the number of trains equivalent in length to a dark green, black, and brown rod, respectively. Generally, students base their explanations on the doubling pattern observed by some students, who notice that for each succeeding rod the number of equivalent-length trains is twice the number of trains for the preceding rod. Specifically, students recognize that there are 8 equivalent-length trains for the purple rod and 4 equivalent-length trains for the green rod. From this they conclude that $8 = 2 \times 4$ gives the number of equivalent-length trains for the purple rod. Similarly, they see that there are 16 equivalent-length trains for the yellow rod and 8 equivalent-length trains for the purple rod, and that $16 = 2 \times 8$ gives the number of equivalent-length trains for the yellow rod. Using this line of reasoning gives the pattern 32, 64, and 128 equivalent-length trains for the dark green, black, and brown rods, respectively.

At this point in the activity it is a good idea to explain to students that in predicting 32, 64, and 128 equivalent-length trains, respectively, for the dark green, black, and brown rods, they have effectively formed a hypothesis about the number of trains that can be formed equivalent to a given rod of any length. In simple terms, the hypothesis is that the number of trains for a given rod is twice the number of trains for the preceding rod. It is important to note that this hypothesis was formed by collecting data, observing a pattern and relationship, and checking to see if the pattern and relationship were true for additional cases.

Verifying the Hypothesis

Now, ask students to draw or sketch on a piece of paper all the 32 trains that they predicted can be formed equivalent in length to a dark green rod. For this activity, have students work individually or in pairs, and encourage them to draw the trains and record the number of cars in each train as you have done previously on the blackboard. Walk around the room, observe student work, and provide one on one help as necessary.

After providing sufficient time for most student pairs to complete or substantially complete the assignment, ask each student pair how many actual trains they were able to make, and record the data on the board in tabular form. Typical results are illustrated in Table 4.3, which presents data from a class of 26 students.

TABLE 4.3 Student Data on the Number of Trains Equivalent in Length to Dark Green Rod

Number of Trains	Number of Student Pairs
33	2
32	4
31	6
30	6
29	2
Did not finish	6

At this point, go to the part of the blackboard that has the sketches of the trains equivalent in length to the white, red, green, purple, and yellow rods. Point out that the prediction for the number of trains equivalent in length to the dark green rod was 32, and that the prediction was based on the hypothesis that doubling the 16 trains equivalent in length to the yellow rod would give the correct result. Then ask students why they think so many student pairs were unable to form the expected 32 trains equivalent in length to the dark green rod.

At this stage of the activity, be prepared for a lively discussion. Many students have an opinion; depending on your degree of encouragement, they will try to explain what they think. Typical responses include:

"There really are not 32."
"I didn't have enough time."
"I forgot one."
"I counted one twice."
"I can't find the missing one."

Actually, many students are unable to generate the 32 equivalent-length trains simply because they do not have an organized, systematic way of constructing the trains. They rely on a trial-and-error method of forming the trains; when this technique does not initially yield the desired 32 equivalent trains, these students are usually at a loss as to how to identify, find, or form the missing trains.

After you make this point with students, you are ready to illustrate for them the value of having organized, systematic ways for collecting information and, in this case, sketching trains. Do so by sharing the technique in the next section for forming trains equivalent in length to a given rod. Begin by showing how the technique can be used to find the 8 trains equivalent in length to a purple rod. Then ask students to demonstrate their understanding of the technique by using it to draw all the 16 trains equivalent in length to the yellow rod. Then, if time permits, they can use the technique to find all of the 32 trains equivalent in length to the dark green rod.

(i) This activity and the next one in Section 8, "Organizing the Data," provide an excellent context for discussing the importance of solving problems in a systematic, organized manner whenever possible. Because the number of trains (32) is relatively large, it is common for many students not to obtain the correct total when they build the trains in a random, trial-and-error fashion. Also because the number of trains is relatively large, many students become frustrated when they have most of the trains but not necessarily all them. They find that trying to identify any missing trains, once most have been obtained, can be tedious, and they tend to give up rather quickly. Consequently, as the rest of the exploration unfolds, I like to point out to students that with a bit of forethought they can develop organized, systematic procedures for collecting and recording data for this (and many other) problems. Doing so, I tell students, enables them to solve the problem and to do so with a minimum of effort.

Organizing the Data

There are a number of ways of forming all the trains equivalent in length to a given rod in a systematic, organized fashion. Proceeding systematically decreases the chances of missing a train or duplicating a previously formed train. In this section, one of the organized, systematic methods for forming trains equivalent in length to a given rod is presented. In a classroom setting, describe the method to students, using the purple rod as a specific example.

Step 1

a. Draw the purple rod as shown in **Figure 4.25**. This step forms the one-car train created by the purple rod itself. This is the only one-car train equivalent in length to the purple rod (i.e., the purple rod itself).

Figure 4.25

Step 2

a. Take the longest rod whose length is less than that of the purple rod. It is the green rod. Draw the green rod as the first car of a train as shown in **Figure 4.26**.

Figure 4.26
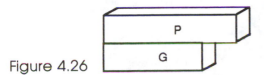

b. Notice the empty space following the green rod in **Figure 4.26**. What is the longest rod that can be placed in the empty space? In this case, it is the white rod, the only rod that will fit in the empty space. Draw the white rod as the second car of the G,W train as shown in **Figure 4.27**.

Figure 4.27

This step forms all of the trains whose first cars are the green rod. In this case, there is only 1 such train, the G,W train.

Step 3

a. What is the longest rod whose length is less than the green rod? It is the red rod. Draw the red rod as the first car of a train as shown in Figure 4.28.

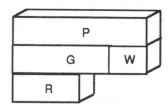

Figure 4.28

b. Notice the empty space following the red rod in Figure 4.28. What is the longest rod that can be placed in the empty space? In this case, it is the red rod, the longest of the two rods, a red rod and a white rod, that fits in the empty space. Draw the red rod as the second car of the R,R train as shown in Figure 4.29.

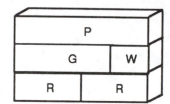

Figure 4.29

This step forms one of the two trains whose first car is a red rod, the R,R train.

Step 4

a. The empty space in Figure 4.28 was filled initially with a red rod, the longest rod that could be placed in the space. But another rod, shorter in length than a red rod, namely a white rod, could also be placed in the space. Draw a white rod as the second car of a train whose first car is a red rod, as shown in Figure 4.30.

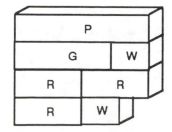

Figure 4.30

128

b. Now there is an empty space in Figure 4.30 following the white rod. What is the longest rod that can be placed in the empty space? In this case, it is the white rod, the only rod that will fit in the space. Draw the white rod as the third car of a R,W,W train, as shown in Figure 4.31.

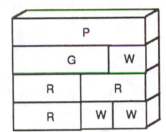

Figure 4.31

This step forms the second of the two trains whose first car is a red rod, the R,W,W train.

Step 5

a. Take the longest rod whose length is less than that of the red rod. It is the white rod. Draw the white rod as the first car of a train as shown in Figure 4.32.

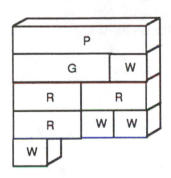

Figure 4.32

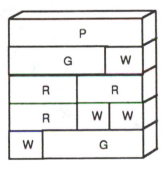

Figure 4.33

b. Notice the empty space following the white rod in Figure 4.32. What is the longest rod that can be placed in the empty space? In this case, it is the green rod, the longest of three rods, a green rod, a red rod, and a white rod, that fit in the empty space. Draw the green rod as the second car of the W,G train, as shown in Figure 4.33.

This step forms the W,G train, one of the four trains whose first car is a white rod.

129

Step 6

a. The empty space in Figure 4.32 was filled with a green rod, the longest rod that could be placed in the space. But other rods shorter than a green rod, namely the red and white rods, could also be placed in the empty space. What is the longest of these rods? It is a red rod. Draw the red rod as the second car of a train whose first car is a white rod, as shown in Figure 4.34.

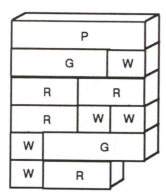

Figure 4.34

b. Notice the empty space following the red rod in Figure 4.34. What is the longest rod that can be placed in the empty space? In this case, it is the white rod, the only rod that will fit in the space. Draw the white rod as the third car of the W,R,W train, as shown in Figure 4.35.

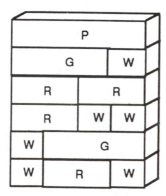

Figure 4.35

This step forms the W,R,W train, the second of the four trains whose first car is a white rod.

Step 7

a. The empty space in Figure 4.32 was filled first with a green rod, then with a red rod. But another rod, shorter than the red rod, could be placed in the empty space in Figure 4.32. It is the white rod, the only other rod that could be placed in the space. Draw the white rod as the second car of a train whose first car is a white rod, as shown in Figure 4.36.

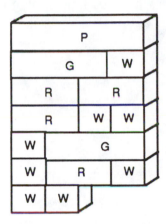

Figure 4.36

b. Now there is an empty space in Figure 4.36 following the second white rod. What is the longest rod that can be placed in the empty space? In this case, it is the red rod, the longest of the two rods, a red rod and a white rod, that fits in the empty space. Draw the red rod as the third car of the W,W,R train, as shown in Figure 4.37.

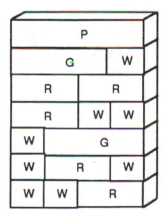

Figure 4.37

This step forms the W,W,R train, the third of the four trains whose first car is a white rod.

Step 8

a. The empty space in Figure 4.36 was filled with a red rod, the longest rod that could be placed in the space. But another rod, shorter in length than the red rod, namely a white rod, could also be placed in the space. Draw a white rod as the third car of a train whose first and second cars are white rods, as shown in Figure 4.38.

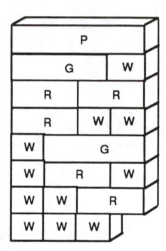

Figure 4.38

b. Now there is an empty space in Figure 4.38 following the third white rod. What is the longest rod that can be placed in the empty space? In this case, it is the white rod, the only rod that will fit in the empty space. Draw the white rod as the fourth car of the W,W,W,W train, as shown in Figure 4.39.

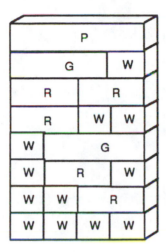

Figure 4.39

This step forms the W,W,W,W train, the fourth of the four trains whose first car is a white rod.

By following the method outlined in these eight steps, you can generate in a systematic fashion the eight different trains that are equivalent in length to a purple Cuisenaire rod. These trains are shown in Figure 4.39. Using this method to form the trains increases the likelihood that all eight of them will be found. When trains are formed in such a systematic way, it is much less likely that one or more trains will be overlooked.

Depending on the sophistication of your students and the amount of time available, you can ask students to demonstrate their understanding of the systematic method presented by asking them to show how the method would be used to generate the 16 trains equivalent in length to a yellow rod. These trains are shown in Figure 4.24. Then, you can ask your students to use the same systematic method to find all 32 trains equivalent in length to the dark green rod.

These trains are shown in Figure 4.40.

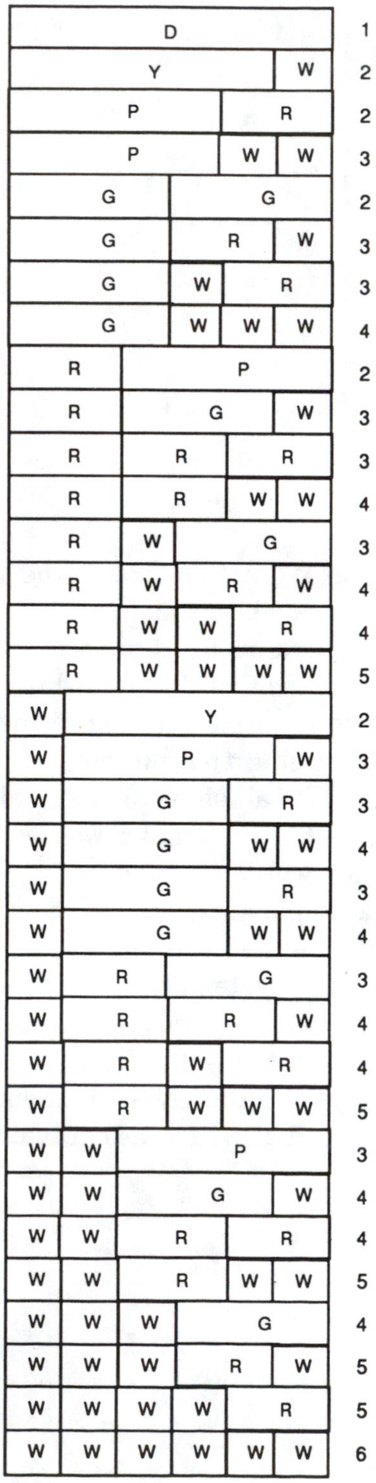

Train	Length
D	1
Y, W	2
P, R	2
P, W, W	3
G, G	2
G, R, W	3
G, W, R	3
G, W, W, W	4
R, P	2
R, G, W	3
R, R, R	3
R, R, W, W	4
R, W, G	3
R, W, R, W	4
R, W, W, R	4
R, W, W, W, W	5
W, Y	2
W, P, W	3
W, G, R	3
W, G, W, W	4
W, G, R	3
W, G, W, W	4
W, R, G	3
W, R, R, W	4
W, R, W, R	4
W, R, W, W, W	5
W, W, P	3
W, W, G, W	4
W, W, R, R	4
W, W, R, W, W	5
W, W, W, G	4
W, W, W, R, W	5
W, W, W, W, R	5
W, W, W, W, W, W	6

Figure 4.40

(i) As noted previously, it is easier and quicker for you to sketch rod trains freehand in two dimensions rather than actually drawing the trains in two or three dimensions. The advantage in freehand sketching rod trains will be particularly valuable if you ask students to use the systematic method developed in this section to form the various rod trains equivalent in length to the purple, yellow, and dark green rods. Figure 4.41 shows two-dimensional rather than three-dimensional representations for these trains. The freehand sketches of these trains took less than ten minutes to prepare following the algorithm presented above.

P

P			
G		W	
R		R	
R	W	W	
W	G		
W	R	W	
W	W	R	
W	W	W	W

Y

Y				
P		W		
G		R		
G	W	W		
R	G			
R	R	W		
R	W	R		
R	W	W	W	
W	P			
W	G	W		
W	R	R		
W	R	W	W	
W	W	G		
W	W	R	W	
W	W	W	R	
W	W	W	W	W

D

D					
Y			W		
P			R		
P		W	W		
G		G			
G		R	W		
G	W		R		
G	W	W	W		
R		P			
R		G	W		
R	R		R		
R	R	W	W		
R	W		G		
R	W	R	W		
R	W	W	R		
R	W	W	W	W	
W		Y			
W		P		W	
W		G		R	
W		G	W	W	
W	R		G		
W	R		R	W	
W	R	W	R		
W	R	W	W	W	
W	W		P		
W	W		G	W	
W	W	R		R	
W	W	R	W	W	
W	W	W		G	
W	W	W	R	W	
W	W	W	W	R	
W	W	W	W	W	W

Figure 4.41

Analyzing the Data

At this point in the exploration, as a result of your work at the board and student seat work, all the trains equivalent in length to the white, red, green, purple, yellow, and dark green rods have been generated. The actual equivalent-length trains for the white, red, green, purple, and yellow rods have been drawn on the blackboard (see Figure 4.24). The number of equivalent-length trains for each of these rods is 1, 2, 4, 8, and 16, respectively. The 32 equivalent-length trains for the dark green rod have been determined and discussed, but these trains have not been drawn on the blackboard, and no mention has been made of identifying the number of cars in each of the 32 equivalent-length trains.

Before proceeding it is a good idea to review the data collected so far on the number of trains equivalent in length to various Cuisenaire rods. Do so by making the table shown in Table 4.4. Presenting the data in this way sets the stage for the next set of activities and helps many students focus their thinking as they look for meaning in the data. You can help students significantly by asking them to look for patterns in the table and giving them sufficient time to think before you actually begin discussing this phase of the activity. A good way to initiate the discussion phase is to ask students what specific patterns they observe from the data in Table 4.4.

During the discussion you can expect a variety of responses regarding patterns discovered by students. Here are some of the correct responses you might receive from students when they look for patterns in Table 4.4.

1. Many students recognize the doubling pattern in the column labeled "Number of Trains." Thus, they observe that each succeeding entry in the column is twice the preceding entry.

2. Some students recognize that each number in the column labeled "Number of Trains" is a power of 2. Some verbalize this pattern as "multiples of 2" as they are looking at the data in the table as illustrated in Table 4.5. Other students verbalize the pattern as "powers of 2" as illustrated in Table 4.6.

TABLE 4.4   Number of Trains Equivalent in Length to Various Cuisenaire Rods

Color of Rod	Number of Trains	Number of Cars					
		1	2	3	4	5	6
W	1	1					
R	2	1	1				
G	4	1	2	1			
P	8	1	3	3	1		
Y	16	1	4	6	4	1	
D	32	1	5	10	10	5	1

TABLE 4.5   Number of Trains as Multiples of 2

Number of Trains		Pattern
1		
2		
4	=	2×2
8	=	$2 \times 2 \times 2$
16	=	$2 \times 2 \times 2 \times 2$
32	=	$2 \times 2 \times 2 \times 2 \times 2$

TABLE 4.6   Number of Trains as Powers of 2

Number of Trains		Pattern
1		
2		
4	=	2^2
8	=	2^3
16	=	2^4
32	=	2^5

3. In the column representing one-car trains, most students recognize that 1 is the entry in each case.

4. Many students recognize that, in the portion of the table representing "Number of Cars," the last entry in each row is 1.

5. Many students recognize that, in the column representing two-car trains, succeeding entries increase by 1.

6. Some students notice, if you start in the column for one-car trains at the entry for the red rod and move diagonally down and to the right, that succeeding entries increase by 1. That is, the entries on the diagonal read 1, 2, 3, 4, 5.

7. Occasionally, some students notice that in the column representing three-car trains the difference between the first and second entries is 2—that is, $3 - 1 = 2$; the difference between the second and third entries is 3—that is, $6 - 3 = 3$; and the difference between the third and fourth entries is 6—that is, $10 - 4 = 6$. Some of these students hypothesize that the difference between the fourth and fifth entries would be 5—that is, $15 - 10 = 5$.

8. Occasionally, some students notice a symmetry in the data in each row of the portion of the table representing "Number of Cars." For example, in the fifth row, giving the data for a yellow rod, the numbers read 1, 4, 6, 4, 1 from left to right. The numbers also read 1, 4, 6, 4, 1 from right to left. Similarly, the numbers in the fourth row giving the data for a purple rod read 1, 3, 3, 1 from left to right and 1, 3, 3, 1 from right to left.

9. Occasionally, some students notice that each entry in the portion of the table representing "Number of Cars" equals the sum of two consecutive numbers in the row above the entry. These consecutive numbers are the one immediately above the entry and the one immediately to the left of that number. Thus, as shown by the underlined numbers in Table 4.7, the 3 in row 4 (the row for the purple rod data) equals the sum of the 2 and the 1 in row 3 (the row for the green rod data). Similarly, the 10 in row 6 (the row for the dark green rod data) equals the sum of the 6 and the 4 in row 5.

Before proceeding to the next phase of the exploration, it is important during this data analysis activity to elicit from students as many of the foregoing patterns as possible. The more informa-

TABLE 4.7   Number of Trains Equivalent in Length to Various
Cuisenaire Rods

Color of Rod	Number of Trains	Number of Cars					
		1	2	3	4	5	6
W	1	1					
R	2	1	1				
G	4	1	2	1			
P	8	1	3	3	1		
Y	16	1	4	6	4	1	
D	32	1	5	10	10	5	1

tion provided by them, the greater is the probability that most students will follow the remaining, final development.

(i) Occasionally, some of the patterns cited here are not recognized by any student. Two patterns frequently not recognized by my students are the pattern of differences in the three-car column (see observation 7) or the pattern of forming entries by adding two numbers in the column above the entry (see observation 9). I actually prefer that no one recognize these particular patterns, as it gives me a good opportunity to provide students with some additional problem-solving insight in the following way. When I ask student groups to generate the data for the dark green rod, the discussion often proceeds as follows. After each student response, I record the correct number in the appropriate place in the table.

Teacher: *What is the entry for one-car trains?*
Student: *One, because all entries in the first column are 1.*
Teacher: *What is the entry for six-car trains?*
Student: *One, because each row in the table ends with 1.*
Teacher: *What is the entry for two-car trains?*
Student: *Five, because the numbers in the two-car column increase by 1.*
Teacher: *What is the entry for five-car trains?*
Student: *Five, because the first two entries are 1 and 5, so the last two entries will be 5 and 1.*
Teacher: *What can you say about the entries for three-car and four-car trains? Are they the same or different?*

Student: They should be the same.
Teacher: Why?
Student: Because the entries read the same from left to right and right to left.
Teacher: What is the number of three-car and four-car trains?

In some classes there are one or more students who recognize that there are 10 three-car and 10 four-car trains. Usually, they reach this conclusion by observing that the total number of one-car, two-car, five-car and six-car trains is

$$1 + 5 + 5 + 1 = 12.$$

Since the total number of all trains is 32, and $32 - 12 = 20$, the number of three-car and four-car trains is 20. Thus, since the number of three-car and four-car trains is equal, that number of trains is $\frac{1}{2}(20) = 10$.

In those classes where no student observes that 10 is the number of three-car and four-car trains, I usually share the preceding line of thought with students. Even though doing so is not crucial to the development in this activity, the logic involved is relatively straightforward and gives students an easily understood example of an argument or justification of a creatively obtained answer.

(ii) This might be a good opportunity to introduce students to palindromes. Any word, number, or sentence that reads the same backward and forward is a palindrome. Some examples of palindromes are

NOON
123321
MADAM, I'M ADAM

(iii) To motivate the pattern of differences in observation 7 on page 138, you might say, "In the column representing three-car trains, the difference between 3 and 1 is 2—that is, $3 - 1 = 2$. What is the difference between 6 and 3? (Answer: The difference is 3—that is, $6 - 3 = 3$.) What is the difference between 10 and 6? (Answer: The difference is 4—that is, $10 - 6 = 4$.) What do you think is the difference between the next *entry in the column and 10? (Answer: The difference is 5, since 10 + 5 = 15.)*

In preparation for solving the original problem of finding the number of trains equivalent in length to an orange rod, you may want to review one last time the information developed so far. All trains equivalent in length to each of the rods, W, R, G, P, Y, and D have been identified, and for each train the number of cars in the train has been determined. Figure 4.42 and Figure 4.43 (on page 142) summarize all this information.

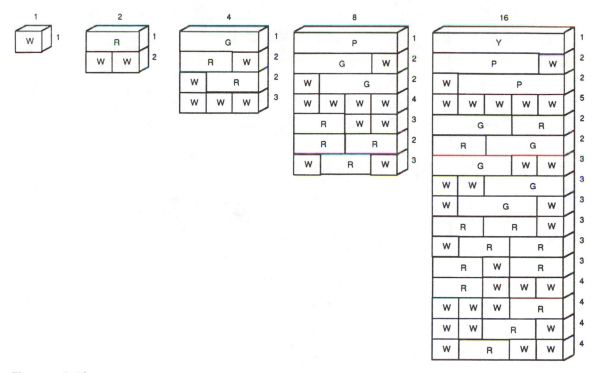

Figure 4.42

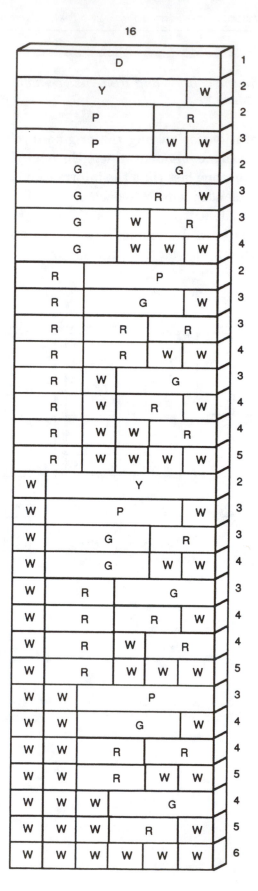

Figure 4.43

A good way to end this phase of the exploration is to ask the class to generate the data for one black rod without actually having them build the trains. They can do so by using the various patterns presented by members of the class in the previous activity. Table 4.8 provides the data for the black rod. Typical student explanations of how the data were obtained (edited here for clarity) frequently include the following.

TABLE 4.8   Number of Trains Equivalent in Length to Various Cuisenaire Rods

Color of Rod	Number of Trains	Number of Cars						
		1	2	3	4	5	6	7
W	1	1						
R	2	1	1					
G	4	1	2	1				
P	8	1	3	3	1			
Y	16	1	4	6	4	1		
D	32	1	5	10	10	5	1	
K	64	1	6	15	20	15	6	1

1. The total number of equivalent trains is 64 since $64 = 2 \times 32$—that is, twice the previous number of equivalent trains.

2. The number of one-car trains is 1 because the first entry in every row in the portion of Table 4.8 labeled "Number of Cars" is always 1.

3. The number of seven-car trains is 1 because the last entry in every row in the portion of Table 4.8 labeled "Number of Cars" is always 1.

4. The number of two-car trains is 6 because the entries in column 2 representing two-car trains in the portion of Table 4.8 labeled "Number of Cars" always increase by 1. Thus, for the black rod the entry is 6, 1 more than the previous entry, 5.

5. The number of three-car trains is 15 because the entry in column 3 representing three-car trains in the portion of Table 4.8 labeled "Number of Cars" can be found by adding the entries 5 and 10 in the row above, row 6. Thus, the number of three-car trains is 15, since $5 + 10 = 15$.

6. The number of four-car trains is 20 because the entry in column 4 representing four-car trains in the portion of Table 4.8 labeled "Number of Cars" is found by adding both 10's in the row above, row 6. Thus, the number of four-car trains is $10 + 10 = 20$.

7. The number of five-car trains is 15 because the entry in column 5 representing five-car trains in the portion of Table 4.8 labeled "Number of Cars" is the same as the entry for column 3. This is true because of the symmetry of the entries in each row. Thus, the second-to-last entry is the same as the second entry, in this case 6.

8. The number of six-car trains is 1 because the entry in column 6 representing six-car trains in the portion of Table 4.8 labeled "Number of Cars" is the same as the entry for column 2. This is true because of the symmetry of the entries in each row. Thus, the last entry is the same as the first entry, in this case 1.

Solving the Problem

The data in Table 4.9 summarize the information collected, organized, and analyzed so far in the exploration to determine how many trains can be formed that are the same length as an orange Cuisenaire rod. Notice in the table that three rows have been added for the data for the brown, blue, and orange rods. In this final activity of the exploration, these data will be collected and recorded in the table.

TABLE 4.9   Number of Trains Equivalent in Length to Various Cuisenaire Rods

Color of Rod	Number of Trains	Number of Cars									
		1	2	3	4	5	6	7	8	9	10
W	1	1									
R	2	1	1								
G	4	1	2	1							
P	8	1	3	3	1						
Y	16	1	4	6	4	1					
D	32	1	5	10	10	5	1				
K	64	1	6	15	20	15	6	1			
N	—	—	—	—	—	—	—	—			
E	—	—	—	—	—	—	—	—	—		
O	—	—	—	—	—	—	—	—	—	—	

Give each student the Activity Sheet shown in Figure 4.44. It contains Table 4.9, with instructions for students to determine and record the missing information for the brown, blue, and orange rods.

The following table shows the number of trains that can be made that are the same length as W, R, G, P, Y, D, and K Cuisenaire rods, respectively.

Record the missing information for the "Number of Trains" and "Number of Cars" for the N, E, and O rods.

Color of Rod	Number of Trains	Number of Cars									
		1	2	3	4	5	6	7	8	9	10
W	1	1									
R	2	1	1								
G	4	1	2	1							
P	8	1	3	3	1						
Y	16	1	4	6	4	1					
D	32	1	5	10	10	5	1				
K	64	1	6	15	20	15	6	1			
N	___	_	_	_	_	_	_	_	_		
E	___	_	_	_	_	_	_	_	_	_	
O	___	_	_	_	_	_	_	_	_	_	_

FIGURE 4.44 ACTIVITY SHEET 4.1: Building Equivalent-Length Trains

Once the Activity Sheets have been distributed, I tell students to fill in the missing data. By moving about the room and observing their work, I have an opportunity to see who has been following the development to this point and who needs one-on-one help.

(i) At the end of this chapter, there is a reproducible activity sheet which you may photocopy for use in your own classroom.

The information in Table 4.10 presents the correct data for the missing entries both on the Activity Sheet and in Table 4.9.

TABLE 4.10   Number of Trains Equivalent in Length to Various Cuisenaire Rods

Color of Rod	Number of Trains	Number of Cars									
		1	2	3	4	5	6	7	8	9	10
W	1	1									
R	2	1	1								
G	4	1	2	1							
P	8	1	3	3	1						
Y	16	1	4	6	4	1					
D	32	1	5	10	10	5	1				
K	64	1	6	15	20	15	6	1			
N	128	1	7	21	35	35	21	7	1		
E	256	1	8	28	56	70	56	28	8	1	
O	512	1	9	36	84	126	126	84	36	9	1

Generalizing the Result

Once the data in Table 4.10 have been generated and recorded, a discussion with students on the methods used to explore all aspects of this activity can be very valuable. It gives students an opportunity to see how solving specific problems can lead to a solution for a more general problem. It is important to note that we have arrived at this place in the exploration by finding the number of rod trains that can be formed that are the same length as ten different rods—the W, R, G, P, Y, D, K, N, E, and O rods. The general method used to determine the number of trains for the smaller rods was to build and count them. For the larger rods, the general method used to determine the number of trains was to observe and extend patterns from previously collected data.

Now, as a result of the information collected, we can make some general observations and arrive at some general conclusions about how to find the number of rod trains that can be formed the same length as a rod of any length, assuming such rods actually existed in the Cuisenaire rod set.

By analyzing and discussing the data collected so far (see Table 4.10) you can motivate students to formulate the following observation and conclusion.

As shown in Table 4.11, each rod in the Cuisenaire rod set can be assigned an integer value (see column 2). This integer value is equivalent to the number of white rods required to make a train the same length as the given rod. The total number of trains equivalent in length to the various rods (see column 3) can be represented as "powers of 2" (see column 4).

TABLE 4.11   Number of Trains as Powers of 2

Color of Rod	Integer Value	Number of Trains		Pattern
W	1	1	=	
R	2	2	=	2^1
G	3	4	=	2^2
P	4	8	=	2^3
Y	5	16	=	2^4
D	6	32	=	2^5
K	7	64	=	2^6
N	8	128	=	2^7
E	9	256	=	2^8
O	10	512	=	2^9

By considering the data in Table 4.11, many students are able to observe a pattern leading to the conclusion that for a rod of any length, n, the number of trains, is given by

$$Y = 2^{(n-1)},$$

where n is the integer value of a given rod and Y is the total number of trains.

(i) As an interesting aside, depending on the background of students, I like to point out the pattern of increasing exponents in Table 4.11. Then I like to ask students to consider the pattern of exponents in reverse, that is, begin with 2^9 and proceed to 2^8, 2^7, etc. Each exponent decreases by 1. Thus, I ask what exponent should precede 2^1. Most students reply, with "2^0," because they see the pattern 9, 8, 7, . . . , 3, 2, 1, 0. I use this as one way of reinforcing the definition that any number to the zero power is 1.

Section F Extensions

Introducing or Reviewing Pascal's Triangle

An excellent extension to this exploration is to introduce (or review) Pascal's famous triangle. For the problem of finding the number of trains equivalent in length to an orange rod, the triangle can be used to find

1. The total number of trains equivalent to a rod of length n

2. The number of those trains with $1, 2, 3, \ldots, n$ cars

Table 4.12 shows the standard way in which Pascal's triangle is usually presented. Each entry in the body of the triangle is located immediately below two consecutive numbers in the row above, and the entry is the sum of those two consecutive numbers.

TABLE 4.12 Pascal's Triangle

```
                        1
                     1     1
                  1     2     1
               1     3     3     1
            1     4     6     4     1
         1     5    10    10     5     1
      1     6    15    20    15     6     1
   1     7    21    35    35    21     7     1
1     8    28    56    70    56    28     8     1
1  9   36   84   126   126   84   36   9   1
```

Clearly, the sum of the entries in each row of Pascal's triangle is a power of 2 and represents the total number of trains that can be made equivalent in length to the various Cuisenaire rods. To find the number of trains for a rod of length n, merely find the sum of the appropriate row of Pascal's triangle. Thus, for example, the sum of the entries in row 4 of Pascal's triangle is

$$1 + 3 + 3 + 1 = 8$$

The number of trains equivalent in length to a purple Cuisenaire rod is 8.

To find the number of one-car, two-car, three-car ... , n-car trains equivalent in length to a given rod, find the appropriate row of Pascal's triangle. The entries in that row represent, in sequence, the number of one-car, two-car, three-car ... , n-car trains. Thus, for example, row 5 of Pascal's triangle contains the entries 1, 4, 6, 4, 1. This corresponds to the number of one-car, two-car, three-car, four-car, and five-car trains equivalent in length to the yellow Cuisenaire rod.

Finding Trains for an O + R Train

In this exploration we developed the formula

$$Y = 2^{(n-1)}$$

to give the number of trains the same length as a particular Cuisenaire rod, where Y is the number of trains and n is the integer length of the rod in centimeters.

Take an orange rod and a red rod and place them end to end to form a train 12 centimeters in length. How many trains equivalent in length to the O + R train can be formed using rods in the *existing* Cuisenaire set? (*Hint:* Careful, the answer is not $Y = 2^{(n-1)} = 2^{(12-1)} = 2^{11} = 2,048$).

Motivating $Y = 2^{(n-1)} - 1$

For the exploration in this chapter, we defined rod trains of equivalent length to include the rod itself. That is, when referring to all of the trains equivalent in length to the red rod, we counted the two-car train of W,W and the one-car train of R itself. Then we proceeded to generate the formula

$$Y = 2^{(n-1)}$$

for determining the number of trains equivalent in length to a particular rod. The number given by this formula included the one-car train formed by the rod itself.

Define equivalent trains so as not to include the rod itself. Ask students to explore the problem of finding all the trains the same length as any given Cuisenaire rod using this interpretation. What formula can they develop to give the number of equivalent-length trains for a particular rod? (One possible answer is $Y = 2^{(n-1)} - 1$.)

Exploring Another Definition of Equivalent Trains

Restrict the definition of equivalent trains to those involving distinct sets of rods. In other words, for the purple rod count only the

P
G,W
R,R
R,W,W
W,W,W,W

trains as being equivalent in length to the purple rod. Do not count the

W,G
W,R,W
W,W,R

trains because the W,G train uses the same rods as the G,W train, and the W,R,W and W,W,R trains use the same rods as the R,W,W trains.

Using this definition of equivalent trains, explore the problem of finding all the trains equivalent in length to an orange Cuisenaire rod. What formula or rule can students find for giving the number of trains equivalent in length to the orange Cuisenaire rod? . . . to a rod of length n?

ACTIVITY SHEET 4.1

Building Equivalent-Length Trains

The following table shows the number of trains that can be made that are the same length as W, R, G, P, Y, D, and K Cuisenaire rods, respectively.

Record the missing information for the "Number of Trains" and "Number of Cars" for the N, E, and O rods.

Color of Rod	Number of Trains	1	2	3	4	5	6	7	8	9	10
					Number of Cars						
W	1	1									
R	2	1	1								
G	4	1	2	1							
P	8	1	3	3	1						
Y	16	1	4	6	4	1					
D	32	1	5	10	10	5	1				
K	64	1	6	15	20	15	6	1			
N	___	__	__	__	__	__	__	__	__		
E	___	__	__	__	__	__	__	__	__	__	
O	___	__	__	__	__	__	__	__	__	__	__

E X P L O R I N G
Combinations with
Attribute Blocks

CHAPTER CONTENTS

Section A The Problem

Section B Unit Objectives

Primary Objectives for this Exploration
Secondary Objectives for this Exploration

Section C Materials Required

Section D Description of Attribute Blocks

Section E Sequence of Activities

Preparing for the Exploration
What's in the Box?
Forming Conjectures
Communicating about Thinking
Analyzing the Conjectures
Introducing Combinations
Answering the Original Problem
Exploring Similarities and Differences

Section F Extensions

Revisiting Combinations
Counting Label Cards
Exploring Attribute Difference Trains
Building a Difference Matrix

Section A   The Problem

The New Age Automobile Company manufactures its Capitol car in several different body styles, color choices, and transmission options. The body styles available are: sports car, sedan, station wagon, and minivan. The color choices available are: white with black trim, blue with white trim, black with red trim, and red with black trim. There are two engine transmission options for the Capitol car: standard and automatic. If customers can purchase a car from the New Age Automobile Company with any combination of body styles, color choices, and transmission options, how many different models of the Capitol car are available for purchase?

Section B   Unit Objectives

Primary Objectives for This Exploration

1. Providing students experience with the problem solving strategies of collecting, recording, and analyzing data; formulating and testing conjectures and hypotheses; and stating conclusions.

2. Introducing the idea of a mathematical combination and how to compute the number of possible combinations of a given set of objects.

3. Helping students develop the ability to discuss and communicate orally their thinking processes used to solve a logic problem.

Secondary Objectives for This Exploration

1. Exploring the notion of what constitutes a reasoned answer to a question in contrast to a guess.

2. Determining the similarity and difference of objects by examining the attributes that define the objects.

3. Providing students structured experience in developing listening skills to enable them to follow verbal arguments put forth by classmates.

Section C   Materials Required

1 Attribute Block set

A small cardboard box with a top

A small sealable plastic bag

A collection of assorted items such as a paper clip, a coin, a piece of chalk, a crumpled piece of paper, a rubber band, an eraser, a marble, a plastic credit card, a dollar bill, and a crumpled paper towel

A small piece of scrap paper for each student

Section D   Description of Attribute Blocks

Attribute Blocks are a set of 32 wood blocks. Each block in the set has three attributes or characteristics: size, shape, and color. There are two values of the size attribute—large and small. There are four values of the shape attribute—square, circle, diamond, and triangle. There are four values of the color attribute—red, green, blue, and yellow.

In the Attribute Block set there is one block for each possible combination of the values of the three attributes of size, shape, and color. Because there are a total of two choices for the attribute of size, four choices for the attribute of shape, and four choices for the attribute of color, the Attribute Block set contains a total of

$$2 \times 4 \times 4 = 32$$

different blocks.

Figure 5.1 shows the 32 blocks in the Attribute Block set. Each block is represented by the drawn outline of its shape. The letter inside each shape outline identifies the color of the block. The letters B, R, G, and Y represent the colors blue, red, green, and yellow, respectively. Usually, the difference in size, large or small, is indicated by the relative size of the block pictured. The large blocks are merely drawn larger than the small blocks.

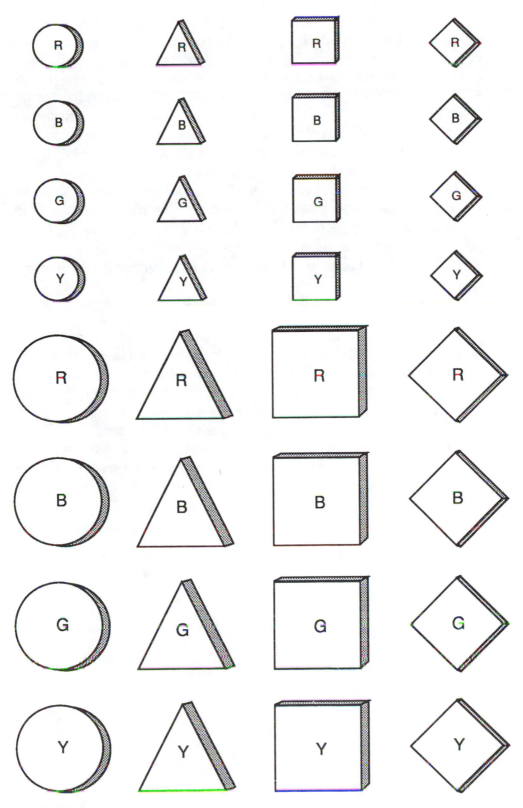

Figure 5.1

Since drawing or even sketching three-dimensional representations of the Attribute Blocks can be too time-consuming in actual classroom settings, it is customary to represent the Attribute Blocks pictorially with two-dimensional outlines, as shown in Figure 5.2. While in this chapter these outlines are carefully drawn, in classroom use, when it is necessary to depict various blocks on the blackboard in a quick and easy manner, freehand sketches are generally the most appropriate way to show the blocks.

In addition to the 32 blocks, Attribute Block sets usually contain a set of 20 label cards, and 3 or 4 elastic strings. The cards and strings can be used for a variety of classification, logic, and problem-solving games and problems. Figure 5.3 shows the set of label cards that is used for various attribute activities.

Notice that there are 10 positive label cards, one for each of the

$$2 + 4 + 4 = 10$$

attribute values of size, shape, and color. That is, there are 2 different values for the attribute of size, large and small, and there is a positive label card for each of these values. Similarly, there are four different values for the attribute of shape, and four different values for the attribute of color. For each of these attribute values of shape and color there is also a positive label card. Also in the set, there is a negative label card for each of the ten different attribute values. These negative label cards have the word "not" on them. Thus, there are a total of

$$10 + 10 = 20$$

different attribute label cards in a set, the 10 positive label cards and the 10 negative label cards.

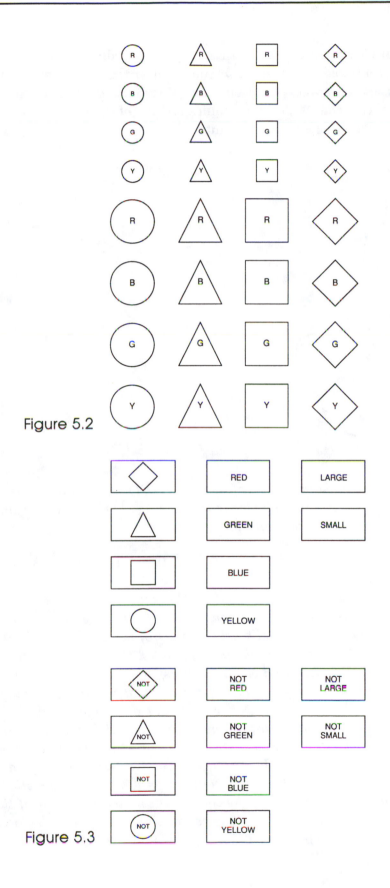

Figure 5.2

Figure 5.3

Figure 5.4 pictures the elastic strings. Generally, the strings are of different colors. However, virtually all of the published activities, problems, and explorations using Attribute Blocks, including those in this chapter, do not require strings of different colors. A single color for the strings is quite adequate.

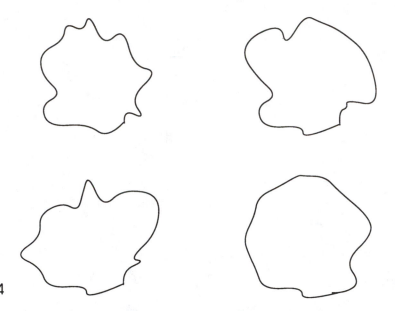

Figure 5.4

(i) If you have a set of Attribute Blocks without elastic strings, you can easily make them using shoelaces, twine, and a variety of other materials.

(ii) As a note of historical interest, the reason colored strings are included in commercially available Attribute Block sets seems related to the original attribute materials developed by the Elementary School Science Project. The original attribute materials, commercially sold as a set of materials called "Attribute Games and Problems," included the Attribute Blocks (with label cards and elastic strings); a set of 60 Color Cubes (10 cubes for each of six colors); a set of plastic tiles called People Pieces, with the characteristics of people on each tile; and a set of cardboard activity cards called Creature Cards, with pictures of various creatures grouped by characteristics. Also included with the "Attribute Games and Problems" materials was a teacher guide containing numerous suggestions of activities for each of the component materials. Some of the activities for the Color Cubes required the use of colored strings corresponding to various colors of the cubes.

Section E   Sequence of Activities

Preparing for the Exploration

From the attribute set of 32 blocks, remove the 12 blocks listed below, which are shown in Figure 5.5.

Large Red Circle	Large Red Square
Large Blue Circle	Large Blue Square
Large Yellow Circle	Large Yellow Square
Large Blue Diamond	Small Blue Triangle
Small Red Circle	Small Yellow Circle
Small Red Triangle	Small Green Circle

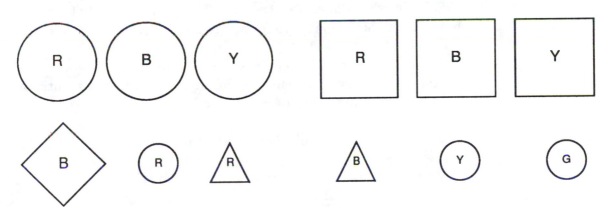

Figure 5.5

Place the 12 blocks removed from the set in a small sealable plastic bag. Then place the bag inside the small cardboard box or, preferably, in your pocket or a desk drawer.

Place the remaining 20 blocks in the small cardboard box. Put them in the box loosely so they will move around and make noise when you shake the box. Also place in the small cardboard box the elastic strings and label cards from the Attribute Block set, along with a collection of assorted items for this exploration. These items might include the following:

paper clip	coin
piece of chalk	crumpled piece of paper
rubber band	eraser
marble	plastic credit card
dollar bill	crumpled paper towel

When all of the blocks, cards, strings, and assorted items are in the box, place the top on the box. You are now ready to proceed with presenting the "What's in the Box?" activity in the next section to a class.

What's in the Box?

Take the cardboard box and shake it vigorously while walking around the classroom. Ask students the question,

"What is in the box?"

Keep shaking the box and walking around the room to allow sufficient time for most students to hear the noise generated by the shaking of the contents of the box. The purpose of shaking the box is to enable students to formulate some idea of the box's contents based on the sounds they hear.

At this point, do not seek responses from students about the contents of the box. Instead, ask different individual students, in turn, the following types of questions.

"Mary, do you think there is any sand in the box?"

"Bill, do you think there is any water in the box?"

"Beth, do you think there is any paper in the box?"

"José, do you think there is any metal in the box?"

"Amalya, do you think there is any plastic in the box?"

In response to these questions, you can expect a range of answers, including "yes," "no," "maybe," and "I don't know." Accept each such answer without comment. Occasionally, after you ask a particular question (e.g., "Beth, do you think there is any paper in the box?"), ask the class a follow-up question, like,

"Could there be paper in the box?"

By asking this follow-up question, you are setting the stage for the idea that, indeed, there might be paper in the box. You might want to actually say this to the class, particularly if some student, Roberta for instance, gives a response of "yes." In such a case, it is quite natural for you to say,

"Yes, Roberta, there might be paper in the box."

Once the sequence of questions, or a similar sequence, has been asked, open the box but take care to keep the contents hidden from the view of the class. In turn, remove one by one the collection of assorted items from the box. Also remove the deck of cards and the elastic strings from the box. Continue removing objects until only the blocks remain. As each object is removed, make a point to focus student attention on the nature of the object. For example, when you remove the dollar bill from the box, you might say something along the lines of,

"You all knew there was paper money in the box, didn't you?"

Or, when you remove the chalk, you might say something along the lines of,

"Can you imagine a mathematics teacher without a piece of chalk?"

In addition to adding a touch of humor, the comments you make as objects are removed from the box are intended to help direct students' thinking to reconsider their original ideas about the contents of the box. The goal is to have students ultimately realize that it is impossible to know, with certainty, what the box contains solely on the basis of the sound created by shaking the box.

(i) Most students find this introductory activity interesting and engaging, and it represents a good way to introduce them to the Attribute Block materials. They enjoy being personally involved by comments such as, "Henry, did you think there was sand in the box?" or "How many of you thought there was a piece of chalk in the box?"

Once all of the assorted objects have been removed from the box, take the sealed plastic bag with the 12 previously isolated blocks out of the box (if you placed it inside the box at the start of the activity). Then put the top back on the box and place the box in view of all students. *Important:* Handle the box very carefully so students are not able to hear any movement of the 20 blocks that remain in the box.

You are now ready to proceed to the activity in the next section, "Forming Conjectures."

Forming Conjectures

In this activity you will set the stage for students to predict and make hypotheses about the unknown number of blocks left in the box. Begin the activity by taking the 12 blocks out of the plastic bag. Distribute these 12 blocks among various students. Tell the students to pass the objects (don't call them blocks yet) among their classmates so that everyone gets to touch and feel at least one block.

Ask individual students to describe the object in their possession. The reason for distributing and passing the blocks among students and having them describe the "objects" is to provide initial familiarity with the characteristics of the Attribute Block set to as many students as possible. Therefore, do not belabor the issue by asking for or expecting definitions or complete descriptions from students at this time. You should expect and accept very limited and specific observations from students at this early stage of their experience with the Attribute Blocks. Here are a number of illustrative examples of the type of responses you might expect from a class. Included with the examples are appropriate lead questions and comments you might offer.

Teacher: What do we call the objects you are holding?
Student: They are blocks.
Teacher: What are the blocks made out of?
Student: Wood.

(ii) Some students may say the blocks are made of plastic. The reason seems to be that so many mathematics manipulatives are now made of plastic, and these plastic manipulatives are often difficult to distinguish from wood, particularly if there is a covering of varnish or stain. Therefore, this might be a good opportunity to engage students in a discussion of how one might distinguish between wood and plastic. Also, it gives an opportunity to discuss the general issue of the texture of the blocks. Texture of the blocks is clearly a characteristic or attribute of the blocks, but not an attribute that can be used to differentiate or classify the blocks since every block has the same or nearly the same texture.

Teacher: Does anybody have a yellow block? If so, please hold it up so we can see it.

Student: (Students with the large yellow circle, the large yellow square, and the small yellow circle should hold up their blocks.)

Teacher: Does anybody have a square?

Student: (Students with the large red square, the large blue square, and the large yellow square should hold up their blocks.)

Teacher: Are all of the blocks the same size?

Student: No, the blocks are different sizes.

With the last question about the size of the blocks, you should expect some confusion among most groups of students. Because of the different shapes of the blocks in the Attribute Block set, there is no true uniformity in the size of the blocks. Thus, even though the Attribute Block set is designed to have both large and small blocks, many students initially have trouble discerning just these two sizes. You may want to spend a few moments establishing the fact that the Attribute Blocks are of two sizes, large blocks and small blocks.

Once you have informally established the three characteristics (attributes) of the Attribute Blocks—size, shape, and color—direct students to bring the blocks you distributed to them to the front of the room. Arrange the blocks in a row on a table or desk in plain sight for all students to see.

TEACHING MATHEMATICS WITH MANIPULATIVES

Distribute a small piece of scrap paper to each student. Then point to the cardboard box that is in view of the students and ask them the question,

"How many blocks do you think are left in the box?"

Suggest to students that they might consider at least two things in trying to answer the question. First, they might consider the information provided by the noise they heard when you originally shook the box. Second, they might consider the information provided by the blocks they see on the table. Finally, tell the students to write on the scrap of paper the number of blocks they think remain in the box. Ask students to record their own answer and not to talk with classmates at this point.

Do not be surprised if some students ask,

"Are there any blocks in the box?"

or if they ask,

"Will you shake the box for us?"

Also, some students may look a bit confused or puzzled.

If students ask questions, merely say at this time,

"I can't answer your questions now, but I will do so in a few minutes."

If you think it helpful, you may want to tell students that you will not shake the box to help them but suggest again that they use the visible blocks as clues in thinking about a possible answer to your question.

Tell the students that when they have written their answer to the question, "How many blocks do you think are left in the box?" on the piece of scrap paper, they should place the paper in a predesignated location, for example on a desk or table. Once most students have deposited their answers to your question, invite a few of them to take the scraps of paper and arrange the information in an organized way. After they have done so, have the students record the information on the chalkboard in the form of a chart (or you can do so yourself). Table 5.1 presents one way in which the data collected from a class of 24 students who were prospective teachers was organized. The table illustrates the range of answers you can expect to obtain from a class of students of virtually any age in response to the question,

"How many blocks do you think are left in the box?"

TABLE 5.1   Initial Responses for the Number
of Blocks Left in the Box

Number of Blocks Left in Box	Number of Student Respondents
0	3
2	1
4	2
6	3
8	4
10	1
12	3
16	1
20	1
24	1
28	1
Don't know	3
Total	24

In addition to introducing students to attribute blocks in an interesting and participatory way, the "What's in the Box" activity enables you to provide students with a foundation for several powerful ideas about problem-solving and mathematics that will be explored in the remaining activities in this chapter.

Communicating about Thinking

An important goal of mathematics study is learning how to use mathematics as a tool to communicate ideas. Equally important is learning how to use language (both written and spoken) as a tool to understand mathematics. The "What's in the Box?" activity helps students experience the use of language in mathematics by providing an opportunity for them to describe the thinking processes they used in solving a nontrivial problem. In the activity in this section, "Communicating about Thinking," you will focus on encouraging students to explain in some detail how they arrived at their answers to the question, "How many blocks do you think are left in the box?"

Begin this phase of the exploration by asking individual students to explain to the class how they arrived at the various different answers they obtained. Some of the explanations you might expect are described in detail in this section. These explanations were actually collected from a group of prospective teachers who explored this unit, although the final statements as written here have been edited for clarity and completeness.

Teacher: Some of you said there were zero blocks left in the box. Why do you think there are no more blocks in the box?

Student 1: When you shook the box, the noise created sounded about right for 12 blocks and the other things in the box.

Student 2: I don't think there is enough room in the box to hold more than the 12 blocks and the other assorted items you pulled out of the box.

Teacher: Someone said there were 2 blocks left in the box. Why did you think there were 2 blocks left?

Student 3: I see 7 large blocks on the table and 5 small blocks on the table. There are more large blocks than small blocks. I think there should be the same number of blocks of each size. Therefore, since there are 7 large blocks and only 5 small blocks on the table, I think there are $7 - 5 = 2$ small blocks left in the box.

When responses like that of Student 3 are given, it is valuable for students if you arrange the blocks on the table to show in a concrete way how the student was thinking in arriving at the answer. Thus, for the Student 3 response, you might place the 7 large blocks in one group and the 5 small blocks in another group.

Figure 5.6 shows one way in which the blocks might be organized on the table, with the large blocks in one group and the small blocks in another group. The first column has the large blocks and the second column has the small blocks. By arranging the blocks in this way, you make it easy to focus student attention on the 2 "missing" blocks. One effective way to do so is to point to the vacant spaces in rows 6 and 7 in the small block column and actually count how many blocks are missing.

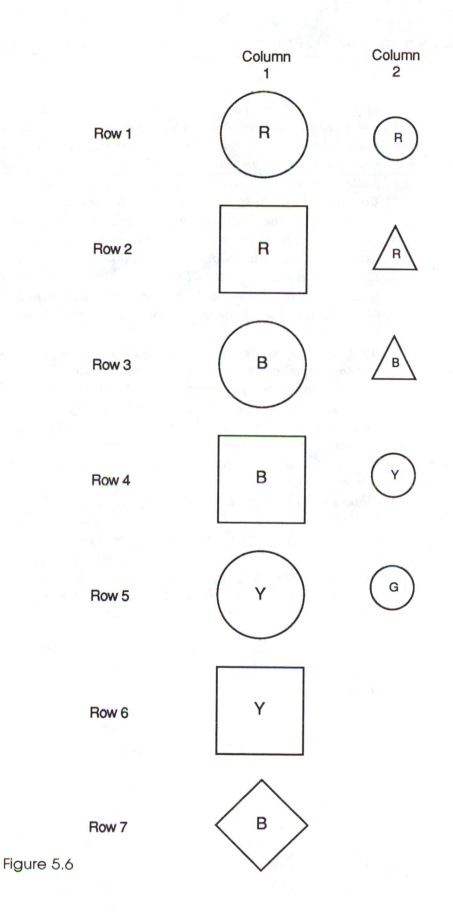

Figure 5.6

169

(i) This technique of organizing the blocks to reflect the explanation of an answer helps students better understand the verbal explanations given by their classmates. Without such a visual aid, many students have difficulty following the explanations given by others. I recommend that for each explanation given by a student, if it is based on something other than an outright guess or non-attribute-related rationale, you should arrange or group the blocks in some organized way to help other students follow the explanation given. Generally, the explanations that should be illustrated in this way, by arrangements of blocks, will be those with a justification relating to the size, shape, and color of the attribute blocks.

(ii) It is very important for you to arrange the 12 blocks on the table to show most of the student explanations given in this chapter. When you arrange the blocks, you should slowly and carefully walk students through the organizing principle(s) you use. This will help them follow the explanation.

I find that having students gather around the table while I arrange the blocks is very effective. Then I run my index finger along the columns and rows of blocks I have arranged while I verbally repeat or point out the attribute(s) that blocks in that column or row have in common. Next, I usually point to one or more of the places in the arrangement where it is evident that a block is missing, and I ask the class if they know what block might fit in that space. This gives students a chance to reinforce their understanding of the organizing principle being used to illustrate the line of thinking under discussion.

Finally, I literally count the spaces without blocks one by one by pointing to each space in order to arrive at the number of blocks left in the box.

Teacher: Some of you said there were 4 blocks left in the box. Who wants to explain why?

Student 4: I noticed that there were four different colors of blocks—blue, red, yellow, and green. I saw 4 blue blocks and 4 red blocks on the table. But I only saw 3 yellow blocks and 1 green block. I think there should be 4 blocks of each color in the set. Therefore, I think there is $4 - 3 = 1$ yellow block missing and $4 - 1 = 3$ green blocks missing from the table. Therefore, these 4 blocks might be left in the box.

Figure 5.7 presents one way of organizing the 12 blocks on the table to reflect Student 4's way of thinking about the problem.

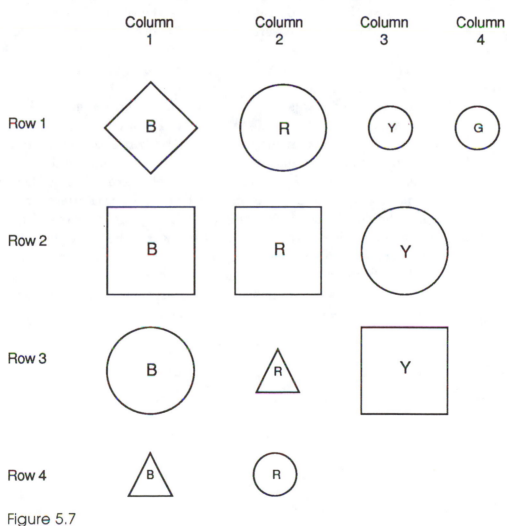

Figure 5.7

In Figure 5.7, the blue blocks are in column 1, the red blocks are in column 2, the yellow blocks are in column 3, and the green blocks are in column 4. Once the blocks are arranged in four columns by color, you can easily point to the four locations with missing blocks. These locations are in the third column, fourth row; in the fourth column, second row; in the fourth column, third row; and in the fourth column, fourth row. By counting the empty spaces, you can readily determine that 4 blocks are missing. Therefore, there might be these 4 blocks left in the box.

Teacher: Someone said there were 6 blocks left in the box. Why did you think there were 6?

Student 5: I'm not sure. It just sounded like there should be a few more blocks in the box. So I thought there might be half again as many in the box as there are on the table. Since there are 12 blocks on the table, I decided there were $\frac{1}{2} \times 12 = 6$ more blocks in the box.

Teacher: Who said that there were 8 blocks left in the box? Why did you think there were 8 blocks?

Student 6: I noticed that there was a large yellow circle and a small yellow circle among the blocks on the table. Also, I saw a large red circle and a small red circle on the table. So I thought every large and small block in the set must have a corresponding large and small partner. Five of the large blocks on the table are missing their small partners. They are the large yellow square, the large red square, the large blue circle, the large blue square, and the large blue diamond. Also, there are 3 small blocks on the table that are missing their large partners. They are the small green circle, the small blue triangle, and the small red triangle. Thus, there are a total of $5 + 3 = 8$ blocks missing their partners on the table, for a total of 8 blocks that might be left in the box.

Figure 5.8 shows one way of arranging the 12 blocks by both size and color. The large blocks are in column 1 and the small

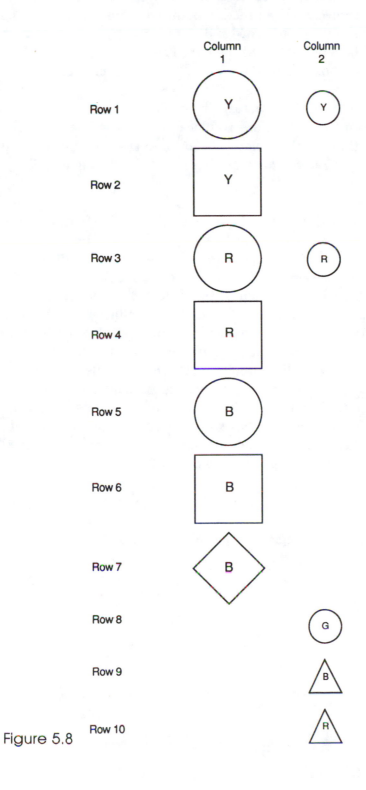

Column 1

Column 2

Row 1

Row 2

Row 3

Row 4

Row 5

Row 6

Row 7

Row 8

Row 9

Row 10

Figure 5.8

blocks are in column 2. Each row in the arrangement has both a large and a small block of the same shape and color, only the size of the blocks is different. Once the blocks are organized as shown in the figure, you can readily point to the locations where blocks are missing in each row and determine by counting that there might be 8 blocks left in the box. The 8 missing blocks that might be in the box are in rows 2, 4, 5, 6, 7, 8, 9, and 10.

Teacher: Someone said there were 10 blocks left in the box. Please tell us why you think there are 10 blocks left in the box.

Student 7: I just thought there were 10 blocks in the box. I didn't have any particular reason for thinking 10. It just seemed like a good number.

Teacher: Several students said there were 12 blocks left in the box. Why did you think there were 12 blocks left in the box?

Student 8: I noticed that the shape with the largest number of blocks on the table was the circle. There were 6 circles, 3 large ones and 3 small ones. So I thought each of the different shapes in the set might have 3 large blocks and 3 small blocks. Since the attribute shape of squares had only 3 large blocks on the table, I concluded that there were 3 small blocks missing. Since the attribute shape of triangles had only 2 small blocks on the table, I concluded that the third small triangle was missing. Also missing were the 3 large triangles. Since the attribute shape of diamonds had only 1 large block on the table, there were 2 large diamonds missing. Also, since there were no small diamonds on the table, the 3 small diamonds were missing. Thus, a total of

$$3 + 1 + 3 + 2 + 3 = 12$$

blocks are missing from the table and might be left in the box.

Figure 5.9 shows one way of arranging the 12 blocks by both shape and size. Column 1 has the circles, column 2 the squares, column 3 the triangles, and column 4 the diamonds. The topmost three rows (rows 1, 2, and 3) contain the large blocks and the bot-

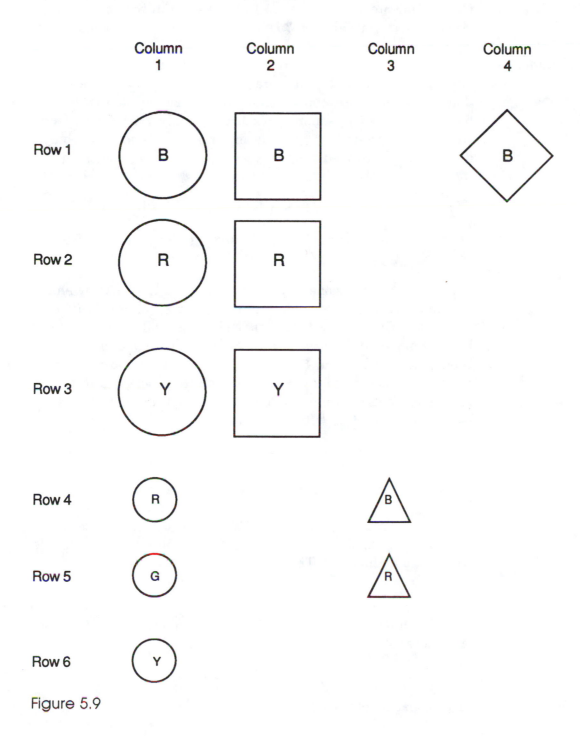

Figure 5.9

tommost three rows (rows 4, 5, and 6) contain the small blocks. Once the arrangement of blocks is placed, you can readily determine by counting that 12 blocks are missing. Hence, there might be 12 blocks left in the box.

Teacher: Other students said there were 12 blocks left in the box. How did you arrive at your answers? Did you approach the problem in the same way?

Student 9: I did the problem differently. I saw that there were a total of 6 circles. So I assumed there were also 6 squares, 6 triangles and 6 diamonds. Since I saw only 3 squares, I concluded that there were $6 - 3 = 3$ missing squares. Since I saw only 2 triangles, I concluded there were $6 - 2 = 4$ missing triangles. Since I saw only 1 diamond, I concluded that there were $6 - 1 = 5$ missing diamonds. Thus, there should be a total of

$$3 + 4 + 5 = 12$$

blocks not on the table. These 12 missing blocks might be left in the box.

Figure 5.10 shows one way of arranging the 12 blocks by shape. Column 1 has the circles, column 2 the squares, column 3 the triangles, and column 4 the diamonds. Notice that all the large blocks have been placed in rows 1, 2, and 3, and all the small blocks have been placed in rows 4, 5, and 6. Once the blocks are placed as shown, you can readily point to the missing locations in the arrangement and determine by counting that there are 12 missing blocks that might be left in the box.

Teacher: Who said there were 16 blocks left in the box. Why was this your answer?

Student 10: I noticed that there were large yellow, large red, and large blue blocks. I also noticed that there were small yellow, small red, small green, and small blue blocks. For each of these 7 color–size combinations of blocks, there could be 4 different shapes—square, circle, triangle, and diamond. Thus, there would be a total of

$$7 \times 4 = 28$$

blocks in a set. There are already 12 blocks on the table. So, there are a total of

$$28 - 12 = 16$$

blocks that might be left in the box.

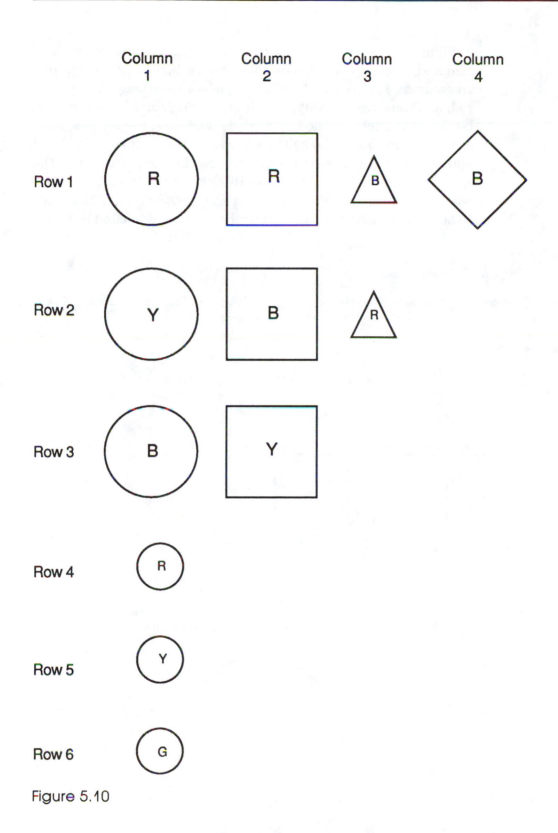

Figure 5.10

Figure 5.11 shows one way of arranging the 12 blocks by both size and color to explain why there are 16 blocks left in the box. In columns 1, 2, and 3, there are large blocks of the colors yellow, red, and blue, respectively. In columns 4, 5, 6, and 7 are the small blocks of the colors yellow, red, green, and blue, respectively. The circles are in row 1, the squares in row 2, the diamonds in row 3, and the triangles in row 4. Once the blocks are arranged in this way, you can readily point to the 16 locations in the arrangement where blocks are missing and count the empty spaces. This leads to the conclusion that there might be 16 blocks left in the box.

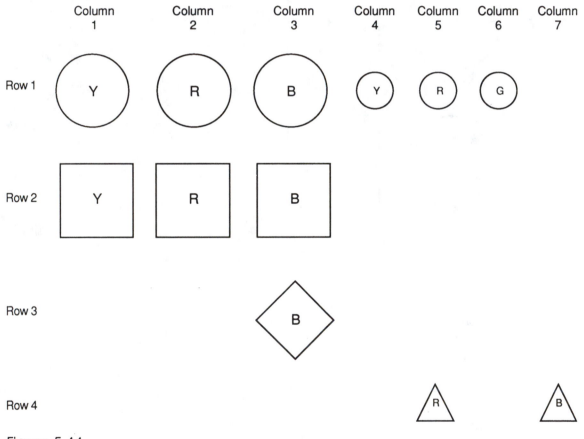

Figure 5.11

Teacher: Someone said 20 blocks are left in the box. Why do you think 20 blocks are left in the box?

Student 11: I saw that there were four shapes for the blocks on the table—circles, squares, diamonds, and triangles. I also noticed that there were two sizes of blocks, large and small. So I concluded that there should be a large and small block for each of the 4 shapes. Thus, there would be a total of

$$2 \times 4 = 8$$

blocks for all of the shape–size combinations possible.

I also noticed that there were four different colors of blocks—blue, red, yellow, and green. So I concluded that for each of the eight shape–size combinations, there would be a block for each of the four different colors. Thus, there would be a total of

$$4 \times 8 = 32$$

different blocks, one for each of the shape, size, and color combinations possible. Since there were 12 blocks on the table, the number of blocks that might be left in the box would be

$$32 - 12 = 20.$$

Figure 5.12 shows one way of arranging the 12 blocks on the table by shape, size, and color. Columns 1, 2, 3, and 4 have the

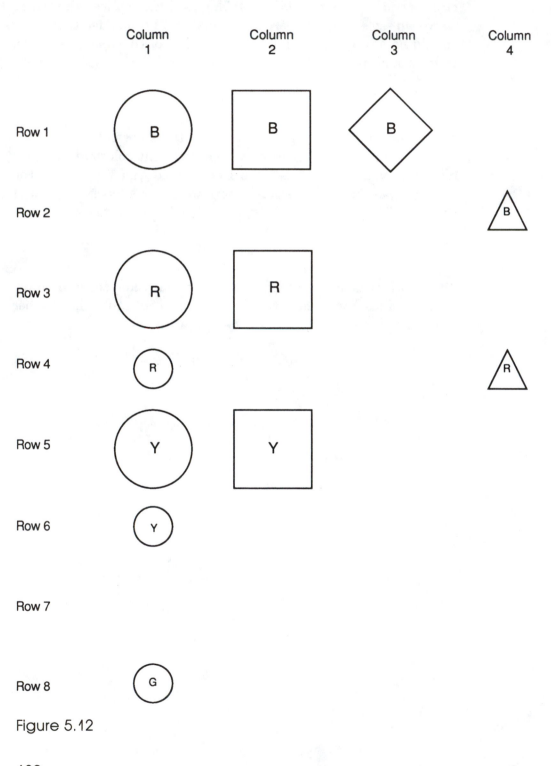

Figure 5.12

circles, squares, diamonds, and triangles, respectively. There are eight rows. Row 1 has the large blue blocks and row 2 has the small blue blocks. Row 3 has the large red blocks and row 4 has the small red blocks. Row 5 has the large yellow blocks and row 6 has the small yellow blocks. Row 7 has the large green blocks and row 8 has the small green blocks. Once the blocks are arranged in this way on the table, you can readily determine the number of blocks that might be in the box by counting the empty locations in the array.

Teacher: Who said there are 24 blocks left in the box?

Student 12: I looked at the 12 blocks on the table and figured that the box probably had room for about three times that number of blocks. Thus, I thought there might be a total of 36 blocks in a set because $3 \times 12 = 36$. Since there might be 36 blocks in a set and there were 12 blocks on the table, I concluded that there might be

$$36 - 12 = 24,$$

or 24 blocks left in the box.

Teacher: Who said there were 28 blocks in the box? Why do you think there are 28?

Student 13: I also saw that there were blocks of four shapes, four colors, and two sizes on the table. So I decided there were at least

$$4 \times 4 \times 2 = 32$$

blocks in the set, one for each combination of the three attributes. But then I thought there might be another shape in the set that wasn't represented on the table. So I added 8 more blocks. Thus, I concluded that there would be a total of

$$32 + 8 = 40$$

or, 40 blocks in a set. Since 12 blocks were already on the table, I concluded that there would be

$$40 - 12 = 28$$

blocks left in the box.

The foregoing explanations illustrate the range of responses you should expect to receive when students explain how they arrived at answers to the question, "How many blocks do you think are left in the box, and how did you arrive at your answer?"

(ii) When you explore this activity in a classroom, it is important to provide ample time for students to talk about the thinking they used in deciding how many blocks are left in the box. Doing so gives them excellent practice and experience in communicating orally about mathematics. However, don't expect initial student responses to be as polished as the explanations given above. Although the responses given do reflect the way in which students actually thought about the problem, the responses as printed in this section were edited for clarity and completeness.

It has been my experience that if sufficient time for discussion has been provided, many students are able to follow most of the justifications given for the different answers. It seems that students often grasp the central idea for how they (or a classmate) arrive at a particular answer but may be unable to express their thinking in clear, concise terms. This is not too surprising given that we place relatively little emphasis on helping students learn how to talk about mathematics. Consequently, this activity is quite valuable because it does help students gain experience in talking about mathematics and learning to formalize final, clear statements justifying their thought processes.

Following each individual student explanation of how an answer was arrived at, take care to say to the individual and class something along the following lines.

"Yes, [student's name], based on your way of thinking about this problem, there certainly might be the number of blocks left in the box you determined."

By making this type of statement after each explanation, you reinforce the idea that there are many correct responses for this problem. This is an important idea to share with students. It will not be clear to many students that, depending on the assumptions made in determining the answer to this question (or many others, of course), there can be a number of different, appropriate correct answers.

(iii) Frequently, when you collect the data on the number of blocks left in the box and invite initial student explanations for their answers, you will have an even wider range of responses than shown in Table 5.1 and discussed in the various scenarios presented. Most students look at the problem in the various ways explained in this section. But other students make a simple counting or other arithmetic error when they actually try to determine the number of blocks left in the box. Consequently, as you walk students through the explanation by arranging the blocks and illustrating the thinking process being discussed, you may discover that the student had the right idea but made a computational error leading to the wrong number.

Since the focus here is on the thinking processes of students, not their computational skills, I generally point out the discrepancy while complimenting the student on the correct thinking approach used.

(iv) During this explanation phase of the "What's in the Box" activity, be generous in your praise of individual students' creativity in thinking about and explaining their responses to the question, "How many blocks are left in the box?" There are many correct responses to the question; in fact, there are virtually no incorrect responses, since a prearranged box could contain whatever number of blocks you might desire up to the limit the box could hold. (An interesting extension question might be, "Given the size of the blocks and dimensions of the box, what is the maximum number of large blocks that the box will hold?") The focus here is not on attempting to determine the actual specific number of blocks in the box. Rather, the focus should be on helping students practice and develop their ability to think about a problem question that has multiple correct responses that are not obvious, and to express or communicate their thinking processes to others.

Analyzing the Conjectures

In the activity in the preceding section, students will have provided a variety of different responses or conjectures regarding the number of blocks left in the box during the "What's in the Box?" activity. (The class data reported in Table 5.1 has twelve different responses.) Now ask students to think about the various answers and explanations that were given. Tell them you want each class member to select the answer they think is most likely to be the number of blocks left in the box. Encourage students to develop a rationale to support their position, and collect the data reflecting their choices in a table written on the blackboard.

(i) A good transition into this part of the exploration is to let students know you are preparing to reveal how many blocks are actually in the box. This is important. Not surprisingly, most students become engaged in the exploration and by now they are very curious about the contents of the box.

(ii) I have always been quite surprised at the level of involvement of the vast majority of students in the "What's in the Box" activity and analysis. In one class a few years ago, I decided to test the degree of one group's curiosity and to see if, indeed, they were really as curious as I thought. Instead of revealing the number of blocks left in the box, I basically told students that we had completed the "What's in the Box" Activity, that we would have a ten-minute class break, and that we would move on to a new problem when class resumed. These were adult students, prospective early childhood and middle school teachers, so I suggested that they take a suitable break and return to the classroom in ten minutes. I then left the room. But instead of going to my office I went to another entrance to the room (there were two doors, both with glass partitions so you could see what was going on inside). Guess what I saw? Several of the students in the class were gathered around the table on which the cardboard box had been placed. One of the students opened the box and placed the blocks on the table. Several students quickly counted the blocks. Then they returned the blocks to the box well before I was expected to return to the room. Of course, this first-hand experience helped to confirm my suspicion that the exploration was engaging for most students and that it motivated a high degree of curiosity on their part.

The information in Table 5.2 shows how the same 24 students who provided the original set of conjectures presented in Table 5.1 now felt about the correct response to the question, "How many blocks do you think are left in the box?"

TABLE 5.2 Follow-up Responses for the Number of Blocks Left in the Box

Number of Blocks Left in Box	Number of Student Respondents
0	2
2	1
4	1
6	1
8	3
10	0
12	3
16	1
20	4
24	0
28	2
Don't know	6

Several observations about the information in Table 5.2 are of particular interest here.

First, it is inevitable that, in this phase of the exploration, some students will believe that the conjecture they arrived at originally is the most plausible, correct answer regardless of any explanations presented by others. This is to be expected and usually reflects the sense of ownership individuals feel for their own work. Interestingly, I have found that even students whose responses were outright uneducated guesses felt this way, at least at this point.

Second, you will notice in the data in the table that there is an increase in the number of students who think that both "I don't know" and "20" are the most plausible, correct responses at this point. When this happens, the former category seems to receive more votes in part because some students become confused when they realize that there are many ways to look at the problem and its solution. As a result, they have difficulty deciding which choice is the correct answer.

The latter category seems to receive an increase in votes because of what I refer to as the "Aha!" phenomenon. Once revealed, it is this conjecture that is appealing and satisfying to most students. The explanation that a set of blocks contains one block for each combination of the four shapes, four colors, and two sizes is seen by many students as "logical" and "obvious" once it is stated by someone else.

Third, the number of different responses has decreased because those students who originally gave answers of 10 and 24 have changed their minds. Now, none of the students think either of these answers is likely to be correct. Usually, as a result of the various explanations given in class, some students do realize that their answer is not very likely to be correct. This is particularly true for those students whose original answer was based on a pure guess, even if that guess had some type of rationale.

(iii) A good technique to use in collecting data on how many blocks students now think are in the box is to ask them for a show of hands as to which of the conjectures discussed in class they think gives the correct number of blocks left in the box. Preface your request for their vote with a statement to the effect that, as seen during the discussions, there are many possible answers to the question, "How many blocks are left in the box?" Then, point out that even though many answers are possible, in theory, there is actually a single, definite number of blocks left in the box. Then ask, "Of all the answers to the question given explained, which do you think makes the most sense?"

At this point in the exploration, refer students back to the various revised responses recorded in Tables 5.1 and 5.2. Point out that the responses given in the tables to the question, "How many blocks do you think are left in the box?" are generally of three types:

1. The "I don't know" or "I didn't try" responses

2. The responses that are nothing more than obvious guesses

3. The responses that are based on some type of reasoned, logical explanation

Let students know that the developers of the Attribute Block set did have some type of organizing idea in order to determine exactly how many blocks would make up a set. In other words, the set of blocks was not manufactured as a random, arbitrary number of blocks. Discuss briefly with students why, in light of this fact, none of the first type of response (the "I don't know," or "I didn't try" responses) or the second type (the responses that were pure guesses) are likely to represent the actual answer to the question, "How many blocks are left in the box?" Be sure to point out that for guesses to be correct, among other things there would have to be an element of luck. In other words, guesses are correct only in those rare instances when the person making the guess is lucky enough to match the guess with a correct answer. The likelihood that a guess will provide a correct answer is low, although it is possible.

> *(iv) With some groups of students, I like to extend the discussion at this point to include a consideration of the circumstances under which a guess is likely to yield a correct answer. During such a discussion, some of the ideas we cover include: (1) the notion that the larger the universe of possible answers, the lower the probability that a guess will be correct; (2) the difference between "outright" guesses and "educated" guesses; and (3) the impact on the likelihood that a guess will be correct if it is an "outright" guess as opposed to an "educated" guess.*

Following the discussion, return to the information in Table 5.2 and ask students to help you refine the data in the table further. Tell them you want to know which of the answers listed in the table should be eliminated as possible, realistic answers to the question. Remind them that they will be eliminating, effectively, those responses that are clearly of the "I don't know" or "I didn't try" or "guess" type. In other words, the answers to be retained at this point include those that were obtained through some type of reasoned, logical explanation.

By this time, many students are able to say which of the responses in Table 5.2 are clearly of the "I don't know" or "I didn't try" or "guess" type. There are five of them: 0, 6, 10, 24, and "I don't know." The "I don't know" responses obviously cannot be correct, and the rationale given for the remaining four answers makes it unlikely that any of them is the number of blocks left in the box. By eliminating these responses, you can focus student attention on the fact that the probable answer to the question, "How many blocks are left in the box?" is most likely among the remaining responses, shown in Table 5.3. They are: 2, 4, 8, 12, 16, 20, and 28.

TABLE 5.3   Revised Follow-up Responses for the Likely Number of Blocks Left in the Box

Number of Blocks Left in Box	Number of Student Respondents
2	1
4	1
8	3
12	3
16	1
20	4
28	2

When you show students the data in Table 5.3, point out that these are the answers to the original question that are most clearly based on some type of logical, reasoned thought. Let them know that in each case, the rationale given had something to do with the various attributes of the blocks—size, shape, and color.

Next, focus student attention on the remaining 7 possible answers in Table 5.3. Ask them to consider those answers and to tell you now which of these possible answers they think is most likely to be the correct answer.

(v) In some classes it may be necessary to review briefly the rationale given for each of the answers in Table 5.3. In other classes, most students will remember a sufficient number of the explanations to be able to proceed with the activity. A good middle ground before you ask students to reconsider the data in Table 5.3 might be to ask them if there are any of the seven explanations that they want reviewed.

Interestingly, many students at this point in the activity will conclude that there are probably 20 blocks left in the box. They have come to believe that there will be a block in the set for each of the combinations of the four shapes, four colors, and two sizes of blocks. As a result, they will conclude that there are a total of

$$4 \times 4 \times 2 = 32$$

blocks in an Attribute Block set and, since there are 12 blocks already visible, there will be

$$32 - 12 = 20$$

blocks left in the box.

Also of interest is the fact that a few students usually decide that 28 blocks are left in the box, if that possibility is generated. These students are persuaded that there will be a block for each combination of size, shape, and color. But they conclude that the instructor has very likely not revealed some shape or color just to make the exploration a bit more challenging.

Once the foregoing discussions take place, conclude this part of the activity by taking all of the remaining contents out of the box and dumping them on a table for all students to see. It is a good idea to invite all students to come to the table to see for themselves exactly how many blocks were left in the box. You might ask one or more students to count the blocks for the class.

As the final activity in this section, ask one or more students to organize the blocks in some way. This final "organizing the blocks" activity is valuable as a way to review quickly with students the various values of the attributes of the blocks—size, shape, and color. Take care to point out that there are two values of size—large and small; four values of shape—square, circle, diamond, and triangle; and, four values of color—red, blue, green and yellow. Usual ways in which students organize the blocks include:

1. Four groups of Attribute Blocks with each group a separate color (see Figure 5.13)

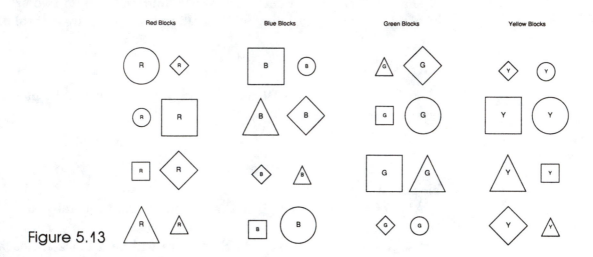

Figure 5.13

2. Four groups of Attribute Blocks with each group a separate shape (see Figure 5.14)

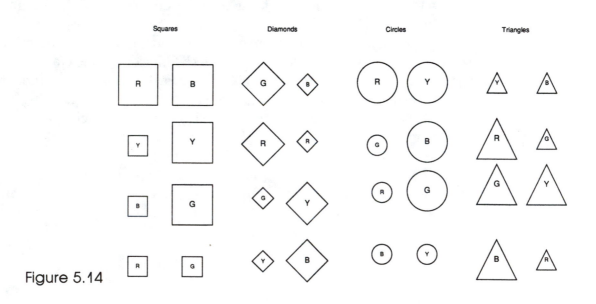

Figure 5.14

3. An array of 32 blocks in four rows and eight columns. Each row contains a different color and each column contains a different shape and different size. Thus, as shown in Figure 5.15, column 2 has large squares and column 6 has small squares. All of the blocks in row 1 are red and all of the blocks in row 4 are yellow.

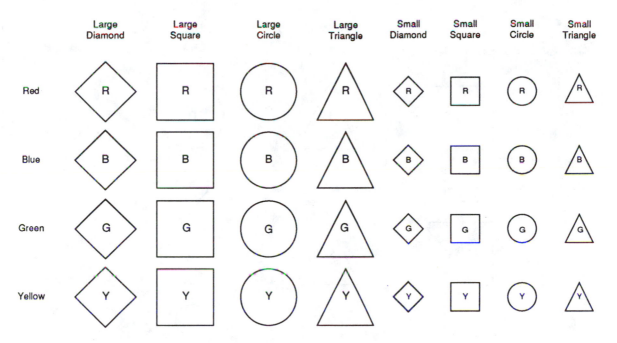

Figure 5.15

4. An array of 32 blocks in four columns and eight rows. Each column contains a different shape, with both large and small blocks in the column. Each row has blocks of a different color. Thus, as shown in Figure 5.16, the first column has square blocks and the sixth row has small blue blocks; the third column has circles and the third row has large green blocks; and so on.

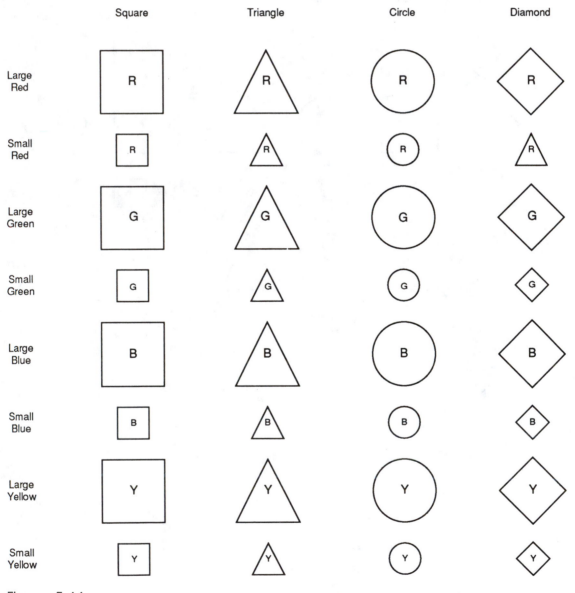

Figure 5.16

Introducing Combinations

Following the opening of the box and verification by the class that there are, indeed, 20 blocks left in the box, focus student attention on two topics. First, review again the components of the Attribute Block set (the blocks, the label cards, and the strings). Emphasize the fact that each block in the set has three defining attributes—size, shape, and color—and point out that each block has other attributes as well (texture, thickness, etc.) but that these additional attributes do not distinguish the blocks from one another since every block has the same (or nearly the same) texture, thickness, and so on.

Next, review with students that for the Attribute Block set there are two values of size (large and small), four values of shape (square, circle, triangle, and diamond), and four values of color (red, blue, green, and yellow). Then show students again that by multiplying the number of values of size, shape, and color (i.e., $2 \times 4 \times 4$) you obtain the total number of blocks (32) in the Attribute Block set. In fact, this represents the number of different combinations of size, shape, and color that can be formed given the two sizes, four shapes, and four colors.

Once the idea of thinking about combinations as a product of numbers is discussed, introduce several other examples for students to consider. Here are a few that you might use.

Example 1:

Imagine a set of Attribute Blocks different from the one here in our classroom. The new set has four attributes—size, thickness, color and shape.

There are two values of size, two values of thickness, three values of color, and five values of shape. How many blocks would this Attribute Block set contain?

(*Answer:* The set would have $2 \times 2 \times 3 \times 5 = 60$ blocks.)

(i) The Attribute Block set described in Example 1 is available commercially under the name of Attribute Logic Blocks. The set consists of 60 blocks with five values of the attribute

*of shape (circles, triangles, squares, rectangles, and hexagons);
three values of the attribute of color (blue, red, and yellow);
two values of the attribute of size (large and small); and two
values of the attribute of thickness (thick and thin).*

*Figure 5.17 shows the 60-piece Attribute Logic set. Notice
that the thick blocks are indicated by the thicker outline of
the shape.*

Example 2:

In Mary's closet there are 3 dresses, 3 blouses, and 2
pairs of shoes. If all these clothing items are fashion and
color coordinated, how many different outfits can Mary
wear?

(*Answer:* Mary can wear $3 \times 3 \times 2 = 18$ outfits.)

Depending on the age and sophistication of your students, you
could develop a unit of study about combinations that, loosely,
means the distinct ways one can select, combine, and arrange a
set of objects.

Answering the Original Problem

The problem posed at the beginning of this exploration can be
thought of as a combinatorics problem or, more simply, an attribute combinations problem. Here is a restatement of the problem:

"The New Age Automobile Company manufactures its
Capitol car in several different body styles, color choices,
and transmission options. The body styles available are
sports car, sedan, station wagon, and minivan. The color
choices available are white with black trim, blue with
white trim, black with red trim, and red with black trim.
And the engine transmission options for the Capitol car
include standard and automatic. If customers can purchase a car from the New Age Automobile Company
with any combination of body styles, color choices, and
transmission options, how many different models of the
Capitol car are available for purchase?"

In thinking about this problem as an attribute combination
problem, the attributes are the body style, color, and transmission
options for the car. Since there are four body styles, four colors,
and two transmission options, there are a total of

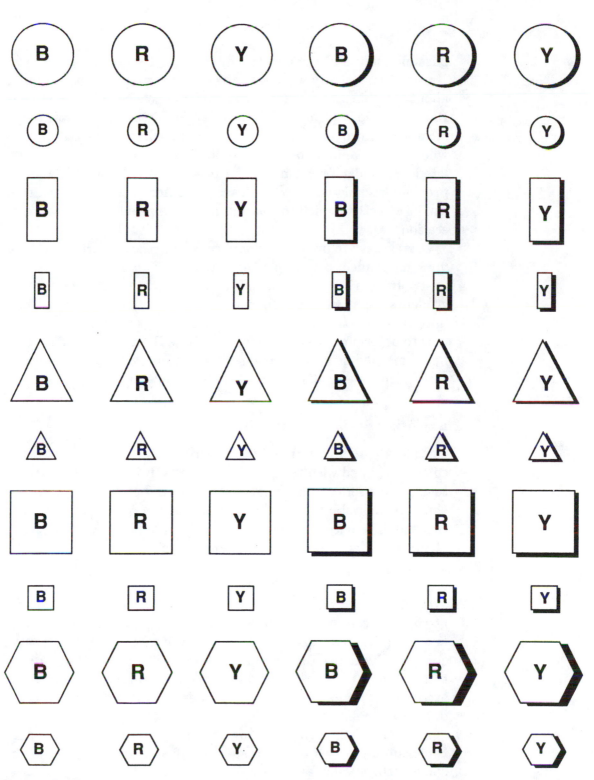

Figure 5.17

$$4 \times 4 \times 2 = 32$$

possible models of the Capitol car.

One reason that you might introduce (or perhaps review) ideas about combinations using problems like those with Attribute Blocks or the Capitol car relates to an important problem-solving strategy known as "Solving a Related Problem." There are times when a good approach to solving a problem is first to solve a related or similar problem. In the process of solving this related problem, techniques are often used and information obtained that can be directly applied to solving the actual problem under consideration.

Giving easy-to-understand and easy-to-present (particularly for younger students) examples of how a problem can be solved by first solving a related problem is a good educational experience for students. One of the side benefits of this exploration with Attribute Blocks is that it presents just such an example. By knowing how to determine the number of Attribute Blocks in a set, one also has a method or approach to solving an entire class of combinatoric problems similar to the Capitol car problem.

Exploring Similarities and Differences

Once students are familiar with the attributes of size, shape, and color associated with the Attribute Blocks, it is valuable for them to explore a series of problems (activities and puzzles) designed to sharpen their ability to organize and classify objects by similarities and differences. In this section of the chapter, two such types of problems are presented—difference trains and difference matrices.

(1) Difference Trains.   Explain to students that in the 32-block attribute set, every block differs from every other block by either one attribute, two attributes, or three attributes. For example, consider the Large Blue Square. Compare the Large Blue Square to the Large Green Square. The blocks are different in only one attribute, that of color. We say these 2 blocks have a "one-difference" relationship.

Now consider the Small Yellow Square. It differs from the Large Blue Square in two attributes, those of size and color. It is the same in the attribute of shape. We say these 2 blocks have a "two-difference" relationship.

To reinforce these ideas of difference relationships, place several blocks next to one another on the table that are different from their immediate neighbor in just one way. For example, as shown in Figure 5.18, place the

> Large Blue Square
> Large Red Square
> Large Red Diamond
> Small Red Diamond
> Small Blue Diamond

on the table in a single row.

Figure 5.18

Then engage students in a discussion of how the first two blocks (the Large Blue Square and the Large Red Square) differ from one another. Notice that they are different in only one attribute, that of color, since the first block is blue and the second is red while both blocks are large and square.

Next ask students to tell how the second and third blocks differ. (*Answer:* They are different in only one attribute, that of shape, since both are large and red but one is a square while the other is a diamond.)

Similarly, ask students to describe how the third and fourth blocks differ (they are different only in size) and how the fourth and fifth blocks differ (they are different only in color).

Finally, tell students that the five blocks (as shown in Figure 5.18) form a five-car one-difference train. Ask them to build another five-car one-difference train at their table. Circulate around the room as students are building their trains to verify that they understand the idea of a five-car one-difference train and can build a correct one.

When you are satisfied that students understand what it means to build a five-car one-difference train, tell them to place the following blocks on the table:

> Large Red Circle
> Small Blue Circle

Small Blue Diamond
Large Blue Square

Then ask them to form a four-car two-difference train using the four blocks.

Figure 5.19 shows how the four blocks could be arranged to form a two-difference train. Discuss with students why this is a four-car two-difference train. Carefully point out how the first and second blocks differ in exactly two attributes, size and shape. Also, point out how the second and third blocks differ in exactly two attributes, color and shape. Then, point out how the third and fourth blocks differ in exactly two ways, size and color.

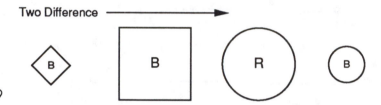

Figure 5.19

Next, direct students to build another (different) four-car two-difference train at their table. Walk around the room and verify that students understand what a two-difference train is and are building a two-difference train properly.

Conclude the introduction of difference trains by instructing students to place the following blocks on the table to form a four-car three-difference train:

Small Red Circle
Small Red Triangle
Large Blue Square
Large Yellow Diamond

Figure 5.20 shows a four-car three-difference train formed by the blocks given.

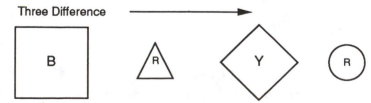

Figure 5.20

Once the four-car three-difference trains have been built, direct students to find and place an appropriate block to be the fifth car of the train. When students have completed the task, engage the class in a discussion of how this train differs from the previous trains. (It is a three-difference train.) Take care to be certain that students understand why this is a three-difference train.

A good way to conclude this phase of the activity is to ask students to form various difference trains. Some sample problems are given in Activity 3, "Exploring Attribute Difference Trains," in Section F of this chapter, "Extensions."

(2) Difference Matrices. Invite students to gather around a table at which you place the following blocks, as shown in Figure 5.21.

Large Green Square
Large Blue Square
Large Yellow Square
Large Blue Triangle
Small Blue Triangle

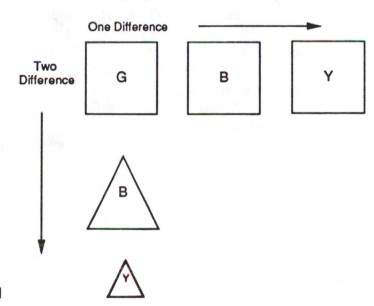

Figure 5.21

Ask students,

"What difference rule is established by the blocks in the row?" (*Answer:* The blocks in the row all differ in one attribute, color.)

Then ask,

> "What difference rule is established by the blocks in the columns?" (*Answer:* The blocks in the column all differ in two attributes, the top two blocks—the Large Green Triangle and the Large Yellow Square—differ in shape and color, and the bottom two blocks—the Large Yellow Square and the Small Yellow Triangle—differ in size and shape.)

Next, in Figure 5.21, point to the location identified by the intersection of column 2 and row 2. (This location is just below the Large Blue Square and just to the right of the Large Blue Triangle.) Ask,

> "Who can tell me a block I can place in this location?" (*Answer:* One of many possible blocks is the Small Blue Triangle.)

Be prepared for considerable confusion. Many students have difficulty recognizing that the block called for must meet two conditions. It must be different from the Large Blue Triangle in one way and different from the Large Blue Square in two ways. It may take some discussion and clarification by you for most students to understand that both the horizontal difference rule (one different) and the vertical difference rule (two different) must be met in placing blocks in this array.

Complete this introduction to difference matrices by telling students to find nine blocks they can place in a 3 × 3 square array in such a way that all blocks on the horizontal are one different and all blocks on the vertical are two different.

There are numerous answers for this activity. One of them is presented in Figure 5.22.

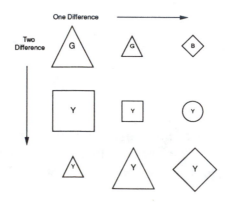

Figure 5.22

Once you establish the meaning of difference trains and difference matrices, there are many interesting problems you can pose for students. Here are four examples.

1. Using all 32 blocks, build each of the following difference trains:
   a. A one-difference train
   b. A two-difference train
   c. A three-difference train

There are many possible solutions for each of the three trains. Figure 5.23 presents a solution for the one-difference train.

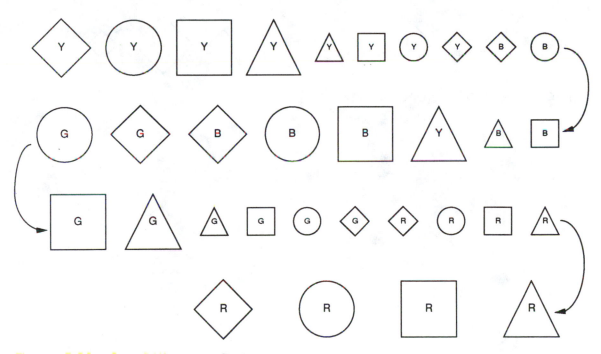

Figure 5.23   One-Difference Train

Figure 5.24 presents a solution for the two-difference train.

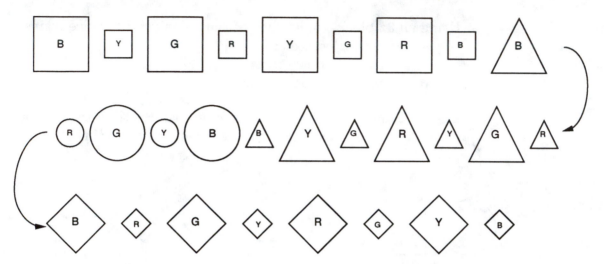

Figure 5.24   Two-Difference Train

Figure 5.25 presents a solution for the three-difference train.

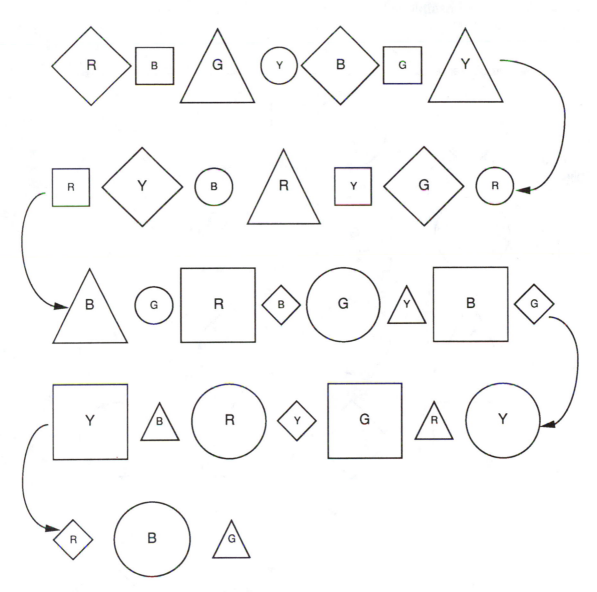

Figure 5.25   Three-Difference Train

2. Using all 32 blocks, build a matrix with a one-difference horizontal rule and a two-difference vertical rule. Figure 5.26 presents one possible solution.

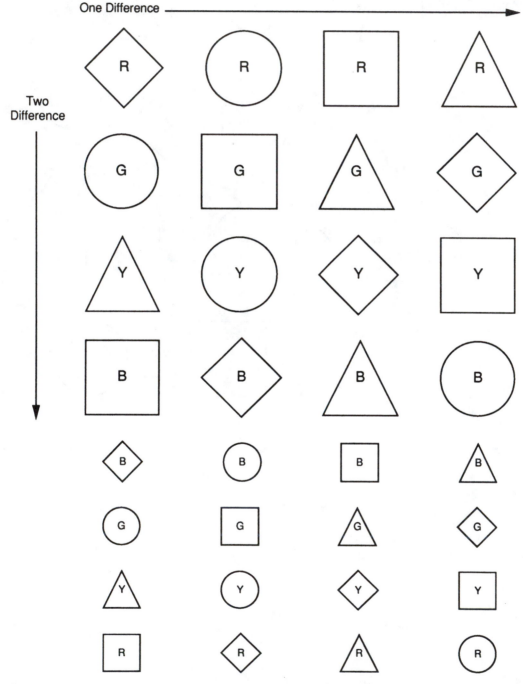

Figure 5.26

3. Figure 5.27 shows a difference matrix.
   a. What is the horizontal difference rule?
   b. What is the vertical difference rule?
   c. Name the two missing blocks.

(*Answer:* (a) The horizontal difference rule is two. (b) The vertical difference rule is three. (c) The missing blocks are the Large Green Circle and the Small Blue Square.)

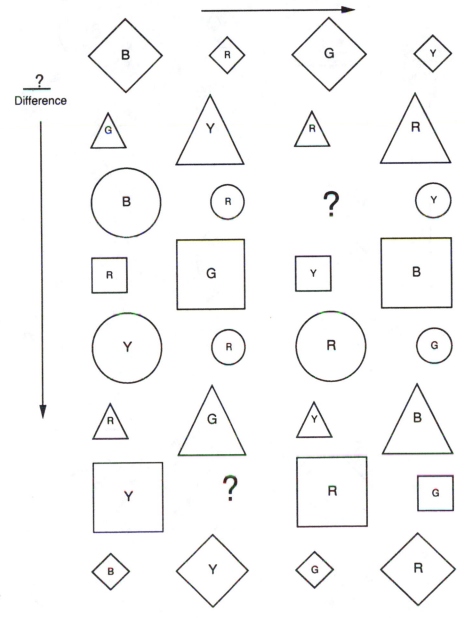

Figure 5.27

4. Using all 32 blocks, build a matrix with a three-difference horizontal rule and a three-difference vertical rule.

(*Answer:* There are many possible solutions, and Figure 5.28 presents one of them.)

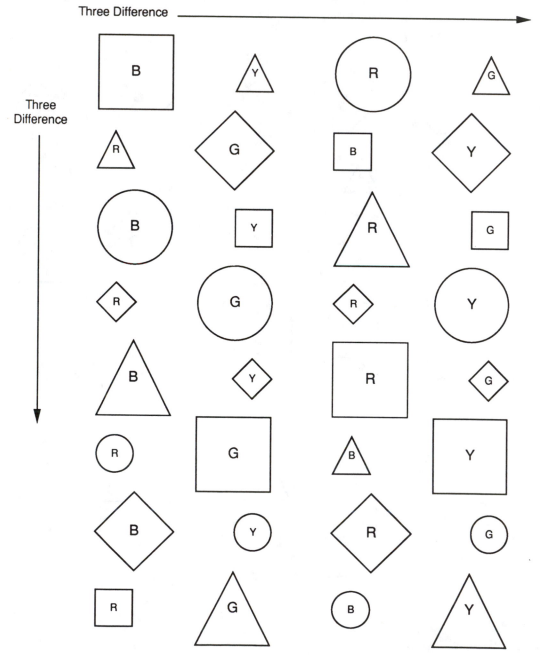

Figure 5.28

(i) Figure 5.28 presents a possible solution for this problem using a combination pictorial/symbolic representation of the answer. The shape and size of each block is represented pictorially while the color is represented by a letter. In actual classroom practice you may want to experiment with the approach you use to represent the blocks. Depending on individual learning styles, some students, for example, may find it easier to work with representations that are completely pictorial in nature. You can present such representations by showing the shape and size as done in Figure 5.28. Then, instead of using a letter to represent the color, shade the shape with a colored pen or pencil so students actually "see" the color. Other students find it easier to work with representations that are completely symbolic. Figure 5.29 presents one such solution. The three letters represent the attributes of size, color, and shape, in that order. The actual value of the attribute is indicated by using the first letter of the appropriate word. Thus, for size the letter "L" means large, for color the letter "R" means red, and for shape the letter "T" means triangle.

LBS	SYT	LRC	SGT
SRT	LGD	SBS	LYD
LBC	SYS	LRT	SGS
SRD	LGC	SBD	LYC
LBT	SYD	LRS	SGD
SRC	LGS	SBT	LYS
LBD	SYC	LRD	SGC
Figure 5.29 SRS	LGT	SBC	LYT

Section F   Extensions

Revisiting Combinations

Purchasers of the New Age Automobile Company's Minima car may choose from among four body styles and two transmission types. They may also select the color of the car. If there is a total of 40 Minima car models, one for each combination of body style, transmission type, and color available, how many colors does a customer have to choose from?

(*Answer:* Since $4(2)(x) = 40$, where x is the number of colors, there are five colors to choose from.)

Counting Label Cards

The Attribute Block set has

$$4 \times 4 \times 2 = 32$$

blocks. The set also has 20 label cards, one for each attribute and one for the negative of each attribute. Thus, there are

$$4 + 4 + 2 = 10$$

positive label cards. Therefore, there are also

$$4 + 4 + 2 = 10$$

negative label cards. Thus, there are a total of

$$2(4 + 4 + 2) = 20$$

label cards for the complete Attribute Block set.

In a 60-block attribute set, with four attributes (size, thickness, shape, and color) and the following values of each attribute:

Size: large, small
Thickness: thick, thin
Color: yellow, red, blue
Shape: square, rectangle, triangle, circle, hexagon,

how many label cards should the set have?

(*Answer:* There should be $2(2 + 2 + 3 + 5) = 24$ label cards.)

Exploring Attribute Difference Trains

Build a 16-car double-decker train. That is, place 16 blocks to form a 16-car train. Then place 16 more blocks, one each on top of the 16 already placed, to form the second level. Use all 32 blocks in such a way that each level of the train has a one-difference rule horizontally. Also, each of the 16 blocks vertically should differ from its neighbor in three ways.

Figure 5.30 presents one possible solution.

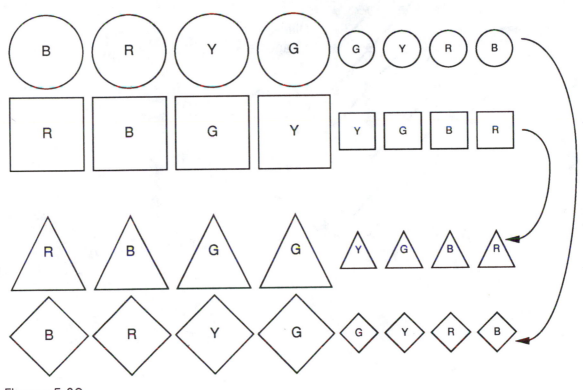

Figure 5.30

Building a Difference Matrix

Arrange the 32 attribute blocks in a 4 × 8 matrix (i.e., in an array of four columns with eight rows). Place the 32 blocks in such a way that each block meets the following three conditions:

1. It differs from its immediate neighbor (up and down) by two attributes.

2. It differs from its immediate neighbor (right and left) by one attribute.

3. It differs from its neighbor along the diagonals running from the upper left to the lower right by three attributes. (*Note:* These diagonals are illustrated by the lines in Figure 5.31.)

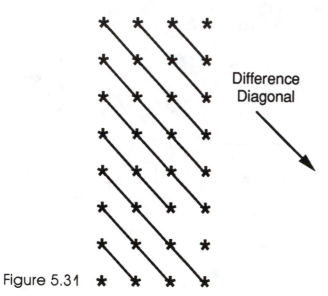

Difference
Diagonal

Figure 5.31

One possible solution is presented in Figure 5.32.

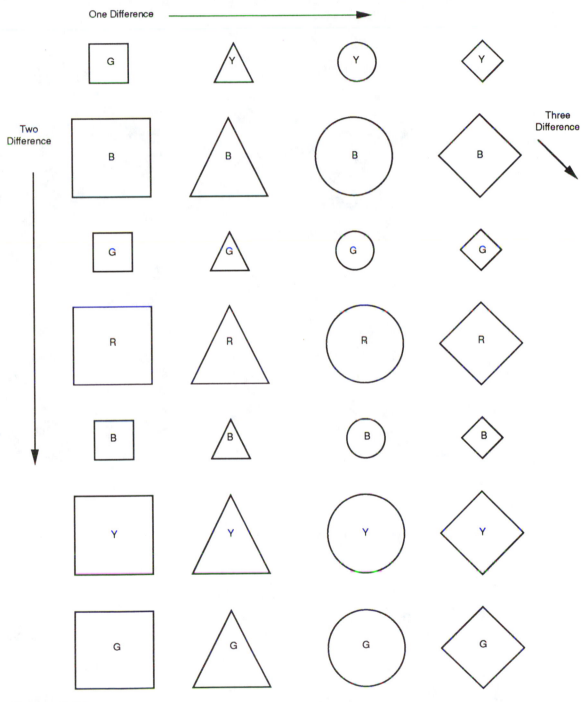

Figure 5.32

P R O L O G U E
Why the Frame-of-Reference Model?

Many teachers have expressed interest in knowing why I developed the frame-of-reference model for presenting teachers with information on how to use manipulatives to teach mathematics. This "prologue" discusses the events that led to the development of the model and explains why I believe the model benefits the largest possible number of teachers.

Educators recognize that concrete materials are an important teaching aid that enhance student learning in mathematics. These materials, commonly called *manipulatives*, are physical, real-world objects that can be used to teach mathematical ideas, concepts, principles, and skills to students. There are two types of manipulatives—those that are commercially produced to be primarily used as mathematics teaching aids and those that are not.

The class of manipulatives commercially produced to be mathematics teaching aids includes such products as Cuisenaire rods, Attribute Blocks, Logic Blocks, polyhedra dice, geoboards, tangrams, powers of 10 blocks, fraction bars, Color Cubes, Multilink Cubes, two-color counters, Dime solids, and pattern blocks. These are products that have been developed and manufactured primarily for the purpose of teaching various mathematical ideas and skills to students. Their primary reason for existing is to serve as an aid in mathematics instruction.

The other class of manipulatives includes two types of real-world objects. In one group are those manipulatives that either occur in nature or are extremely inexpensive manufactured products. Examples of such manipulatives include string, beans, coins, pebbles, tongue depressors, and paper. In the other group of manipulatives are those commercially manufactured products that have possible educational applications but exist primarily for some other purpose. Examples of such manipulatives include Tinker Toys, Legos, jigsaw puzzles, and children's building blocks. Both types of real-world objects, the naturally occurring and the noneducational manufactured products, can be used in some creative ways to teach selected mathematical topics. But none of these manipulatives were originally produced for that purpose. They exist in the culture for other reasons than serving as mathematics instructional aids.

In the past twenty-five years, the demand for the use of manipulatives in mathematics teaching has grown significantly. This is particularly true for the commercially manufactured products that have been developed specifically as aids in mathematics instruction. As demand has increased, so too has the availability of appropriate manipulative products. In the early 1960s, there were a few small start-up companies developing, manufacturing, and selling a limited number of manipulatives as supplementary resources. Today there are many such suppliers. The largest of these—companies like Cuisenaire Company of America, Creative Publications, Dale Seymour Publications, Didax Educational Resources, Nasco, and ETA—are multimillion-dollar businesses with extensive product lines that may include the mathematics manipulatives, student curriculum materials for classroom use, teacher resource books, computer software, videotapes, and a variety of other instructional aids.

Once regarded as supplementary resource materials in the classroom, commercially produced mathematics manipulatives are today viewed as central, core instructional aids in quality school mathematics programs. Most major publishers of elementary school mathematics books now offer or at least recommend that mathematics manipulative kits be included as integral components with their textbook series. In recent years several large states, notably California and Texas, have mandated that all elementary school mathematics programs in their states must adopt mathematics manipulatives components.

Unfortunately, the dramatic increase in the supply and demand for commercially manufactured mathematics manipulatives has not yet resulted in significant changes or improvements in many school mathematics instructional programs. There is even some anecdotal information to suggest that as mathematics manipulatives have become more widely available, their effective use in instruction may actually have decreased. It is not uncommon to find schools and individual teachers with adequate manipulative supplies that are stored in closets and only rarely used. Also, the incidence of improper use or underutilization of commercially manufactured mathematics manipulatives seems to be on the increase.

Why are commercially manufactured mathematics manipulatives sitting on shelves in closets or being improperly used in instructional programs? After twenty-some years in teacher education, I am convinced that the dominant reason for improper use or underutilization of commercially manufactured mathematics manipulatives (hereafter referred to solely as manipulatives) is primarily the result of inadequate initial preparation and follow-on support given to most teachers on the use of these manipulatives. Let me explain.

The classroom teachers who were the early adopters of manipulatives in the late 1960s and 1970s were, on the whole, a highly motivated group of innovators. They tended to be extraordinary individuals who were interested in exploring new ideas in their search for ways to improve their effectiveness as teachers. They had innate enthusiasm, motivation, and ability to understand the power of manipulatives as instructional aids. With little additional education, they understood the mathematics content embodied by various manipulatives and the best methods for teaching school mathematics topics to children using manipulatives.

These early innovators required little specialized training before they were willing to use manipulatives in their classrooms. Most of them began using manipulatives in the classroom in experimental, trial ways after one or two introductory workshop experiences. As a result of their successes, these individuals served as the first generation of teachers to champion this new class of instructional aids. They helped set the stage for manipulatives to play an increasingly prominent role in the instructional program of many schools. One of their most effective contributions was to interest and encourage a second group of teachers to try manipulatives. These second-round adopters were people who possessed many of the characteristics of the early adopters.

Frequently, both the early and second-round adopters had the good fortune of learning about manipulatives by working with the very people who had invented or created the manipulatives—people like William Hull, creator of Attribute Blocks; Zolten Dienes, creator of Multibase Blocks; and Pat Davison and Al Bennett, creators of Chip Trading Materials and Fraction Bars. Most of these inventors and creators were dynamic, intelligent, personable, dedicated professionals who served as both prophet and mentor to many of the early and second-round adopters. In turn, these early users of manipulatives effectively became the disciples of the pioneer inventor/creators and their professional associates. As disciples or strong supporters, these earliest users worked closely with the inventor/creators, their professional associates, and others to implement manipulatives in their own classrooms and to spread the word about the educational value and potential of manipulatives to others, the later adopters.

In addition to being introduced to manipulatives by the actual inventor/creators, the early and second-round adopters had other advantages that helped motivate them and fire their enthusiasm for manipulatives and their effectiveness in stimulating the interest of others, the later adopters. These included the opportunities to enhance their knowledge of manipulatives by working and studying directly with younger college and university teacher/researchers who were destined to become the generation of mathematics educators who played the major role in developing, leading, and promoting the mathematics manipulatives movement.

In the late 1960s and through the 1970s, a large group of mathematics educators devoted considerable time, energy, and effort to various research, curriculum development, and implementation projects directly related to the integration of manipulatives in the classroom. These college and university mathematics educators included such persons as Dr. William Fitzgerald of Michigan State University, co-author of *Laboratory Manual for Elementary Mathematics* (Boston: Prindle, Weber & Schmidt, 1969); Dr. Carole E. Greenes and Dr. Robert Willcutt of Boston University, who, with me, co-authored *Problem Solving in the Mathematics Laboratory* (Boston: Prindle, Weber & Schmidt, 1972), and Dr. Robert E. Reys of the University of Missouri and Dr. Thomas R. Post of the University of Minnesota, co-authors of *A Mathematics Laboratory in the Classroom* (Boston: Prindle, Weber & Schmidt, 1973). Each of these men and women, together with the scores of others in colleges and universities supporting the manipulatives movement, also served as both prophets and mentors for the earliest serious users of manipulatives in schools.

These mathematics educators helped move the mathematics manipulatives movement forward in many ways. They conducted staff development workshops for teachers; delivered papers and ran sessions at meetings of organizations like the National Council of Teachers of Mathematics; wrote teacher and student curriculum materials, books, research reports, and grants; integrated mathematics manipulatives into their undergraduate and graduate mathematics and teacher education courses; and supervised the research of their doctoral students. These educators had a major influence on the emerging mathematics manipulatives movement and served as ideal mentors for the classroom-based personnel who were the earliest users of manipulatives in the classroom.

Ultimately, the earliest adopters of manipulatives in the classroom and the mathematics educator mentors with whom they worked and studied generated enough interest and enthusiasm in the profession for the manipulatives movement to gain significant momentum—so much so that the later adopters, the millions of teachers in U.S. schools who were not yet using manipulatives, were ready at least to try manipulatives in their classrooms.

It was at this time that the manipulatives movement faltered, stumbled, and almost failed. The early adopters benefited from their relationship with the earliest developers and pioneers of the manipulative materials movement. There is something special about being caught up in the excitement of new ideas and emerging research. Equally important, the earliest adopters possessed the knowledge, initiative, and leadership ability to incorporate manipulatives into the school academic program with little initial or follow-on support. They believed that manipulatives were a powerful teaching aid and did not have to be convinced of their potential value. Moreover, they had the requisite interest, motivation, and skills to discover for themselves, with minimal help, how to incorporate manipulatives in their instructional programs. In short, they required minimal formal preparation to use manipulatives.

Once introduced to mathematics manipulatives, these early adopters often became so dedicated to the cause that they would devote extraordinary personal resources, both time and money, to learning more about the use of mathematics manipulatives in their classrooms. Often they actually purchased the manipulatives to use in their classes from their own funds. To these innovators, mathematics manipulatives became the tangible vehicle for improving the mathematics education of all students in schools. Frequently these early adopters ceased being traditional elementary classroom teachers, at least in the sense of continuing to teach all the major subject areas (science, math, language arts, social studies) equally in a self-contained classroom. Many became resource teachers, specialists, part-time teachers, or part-time staff developers. Those that remained in the classroom often redistributed their teaching efforts in such a way as to give greater emphasis and more time to teaching mathematics with manipulatives. And these innovators led the way in increasing the number of effective ways in which mathematics manipulatives could be used in teaching nontraditional elementary school topics such as probability, statistics, and problem solving.

Whatever their role in the schools, the earliest adopters established and maintained high standards of excellence in using manipulatives in the classroom—standards of excellence that all teachers should emulate. Their instructional and curriculum leadership successes ultimately led to increased numbers of teachers who became interested, eager, and willing (or who were forced) to use manipulatives in the mathematics instructional program. Herein developed the specific problem.

As ever-increasing numbers of teachers began to use or desire to use manipulatives, the nature and depth of the education and training needed to prepare these teachers changed significantly. These later adopters, good as many of them were as teachers, needed more extensive training in order to utilize manipulatives in the classroom. Often they had relatively weak backgrounds in mathematics and required additional mathematics preparation in order to appreciate the many topics manipulatives could be used to teach. Frequently, they wanted and needed to be convinced of why this new innovation was worth adopting, and they were less willing to incorporate manipulatives than the early adopters had been. Understandably, they were unwilling to spend their own resources, whether of time or money, to buy manipulatives or learn how to use them effectively in instruction. In other words, these later adopters needed in-depth preparation and extensive follow-on help to ensure the successful implementation of manipulatives in their classrooms.

As increasing numbers of teachers needed preparation to use manipulatives, resources were stretched to the limit. It was barely possible to obtain sufficient resources for introductory workshops and the purchase of modest amounts of manipulatives for classroom use. The idea of providing in-depth preparation and follow-on help for these later adopters, though worthwhile, was impractical and financially unattainable. The numbers of teachers to be involved was staggering, and resources to provide proper education and training for literally millions of individuals were just not available.

Given this reality, one possibility was to delay the adoption of manipulatives until such time as the resources actually needed were available. That did not happen, however, and nationwide a different approach emerged, more by accident than by design. Simply put, most school districts decided to forge ahead with very modest investments in manipulatives and teacher preparation in the apparent belief that some use of manipulatives was better than none. Large numbers of teachers were given introductory workshop experiences, and modest quantities of manipulatives were purchased. Then the teachers were encouraged to begin incorporating the manipulatives into their instructional programs. In part, this approach was due to the known lack of resources. But the approach was also utilized in the belief that many of the later adopters would be as successful in using manipulatives with this limited type of preparation as were the earlier adopters. It was believed, or at least articulated, that the early and later adopters were all "experienced" teachers. Thus, what the early adopters could do, surely the later adopters could and would also do.

In hindsight, the approach that emerged appears to have been seriously flawed. Most of the later adopters were good teachers, but many did not possess the same characteristics as the early adopters. This group usually did not have the benefit of the "halo effect" of working and studying with the inventors and pioneers of the movement. And, although they were quite competent as teachers, many were not naturally gifted in mathematics or the teaching of mathematics. They really needed in-depth help in order to achieve the same levels of success as the early adopters. But instead of in-depth experiences with manipulatives and thoughtful follow-on programs of support, this ever-increasing number of later adopters often received only cursory introductory workshops. As already noted, it was thought that they would react much as did the early adopters. In other words, it was believed (or hoped) that these teachers would exhibit the same degree of enthusiasm, mastery, dedication, and success as the early adopters.

Unfortunately, we do not live in an ideal world in which all teachers possess the motivation, skills, and talents of the early adopters. The majority of teachers are quite capable, qualified, and competent but are by no means possessed by the fervor, dedication, or ability to implement new ideas that characterizes the true early adopters of most innovations, especially mathematics manipulatives. Herein lies the source of the problem. There is something radically wrong with the way we have helped noninnovators to utilize manipulatives in the past and how we continue to help them today.

Typically, the classroom teachers who needed to use manipulatives (or were told to use them) had relatively weak content backgrounds in mathematics. This is not a criticism, but a statement of fact. There are many classroom teachers who have an inadequate mathematics background for one reason or another. They may dislike mathematics, or they may have been poor students of mathematics, or perhaps they just did not take enough math courses in their educational programs. Some teachers consider mathematics one of the least desirable subjects to teach. As a result of both their weak content backgrounds and their negative attitudes toward mathematics, they view the task of teaching mathematics in general with understandable trepidation and caution. And they view the task of teaching mathematics in innovative ways with little enthusiasm, particularly when virtually no substantive resources are available to help them with the task.

These teachers, many of whom were the later adopters, recognized in the late 1970s and 1980s that incorporating manipulatives called for a major effort on their part and that "new" thinking would be needed to improve their ability to teach mathematics.

But they were unable then—and many remain unable today—to find the resources necessary to support such efforts on their part. How will these teachers learn to use manipulatives? What follow-on help will they be given for incorporating manipulatives in the classroom? Who will help them design lessons and units for their particular classroom needs?

It is not surprising, then, that these potential later adopters were reluctant to embrace mathematics manipulatives or any innovation (technology, for another good example) with the same enthusiasm as the early adopters. What sense did it make to use manipulatives as a replacement for or a supplement to more traditional teaching aids and methods that they had already mastered? Most teachers of elementary, middle school, and junior high school mathematics rely heavily on the textbook series with its extensive support materials in the form of teacher guides complete with lesson plans, prewritten tests, student activity booklets, staff development programs for teachers provided by the publishers and adopting school divisions, and the like. These traditional textbook support materials create a formidable barrier for change. Are such aids available for teachers who use manipulatives?

The problem is exacerbated today by the usual methods used to provide training for teachers in the use of mathematics manipulatives. Most often teachers are given introductory workshops on particular mathematics manipulatives, or they take overview courses on teaching methods surveying a variety of mathematics manipulatives and how to use them in the classroom. Then, they are given a supply of mathematics manipulatives, perhaps a few resource books with ideas for student activities, and off they go to incorporate mathematics manipulatives into the curriculum. While these experiences are somewhat helpful, they are hardly sufficient. And that should not surprise us!

To use manipulatives properly, teachers must have a good understanding of three things:

1. What is the content embodied in the manipulative?

2. Which specific activities can be used to teach the content with the manipulative?

3. What teaching methods are effective for teaching the content with the manipulative?

It is the rare person who can acquire the requisite knowledge in these three areas after only introductory or cursory inservice experiences.

After over twenty years of working with teachers, I believe that to use manipulatives effectively, most teachers need to design and prepare suitable materials for their own classrooms, in the form of lessons and units that incorporate manipulatives in the teaching of various mathematics topics. In order to do this, these teachers need extensive hands-on exploration with the materials themselves before they ever begin to think about using manipulatives in the classroom. They need to understand the mathematics embodied in various manipulatives, and they need to see, through the experience of exploring manipulatives themselves, how the manipulatives can be used to teach various mathematics content or other instructional objectives. Finally, they need to see some specific examples of the type of lessons and units that can be prepared and used to teach mathematics successfully using manipulatives. Such sample materials become, for the teacher, a frame-of-reference, or guide, to the types of activities they should consider preparing for their own classes.

The requisite knowledge and experience required by teachers interested in utilizing manipulatives are difficult, if not impossible, to provide in traditional inservice workshops or courses that offer the typical overview and introductory exposure to manipulatives. Providing specific workshops and courses for a proper in-depth exploration of mathematics manipulatives and how to use them may not always be practical or feasible. Frequently, instructional personnel are not available to offer such in-depth experiences, and there are financial and time limitations for supporting in-depth teacher training to use mathematics manipulatives.

In order for teachers to be able to use manipulatives effectively, we must find and provide alternative ways for them to acquire the requisite knowledge and experience with the content embodied in mathematics manipulatives, so that they know which activities to use to teach that content with mathematics manipulatives and which methods to use to teach that content using the mathematics manipulatives.

To provide just one such alternative, I developed and tested the frame-of-reference model. Briefly, the idea was to prepare sample lessons or scripts specifically for the later adopter teachers. The scripts would effectively describe exactly how a mathematics topic might be presented in a classroom with manipulatives. The presentation would be thorough from beginning to end. Extensive figures and drawings would be used to clarify ideas and present data and answers. Specific examples of teaching methods would be given, and expected student responses to various questions would be included.

The idea behind the frame-of-reference model was not to give teachers a script that they in turn could copy for classroom presentation purposes, although that certainly could be done as an initial step for teachers who wanted to experiment. Instead, the model was developed as a way to give teachers all the information a novice would need to begin thinking about how to incorporate the use of manipulatives to teach mathematics topics. From the beginning, it has been the goal of the model to encourage teachers to follow the script for their own learning purposes but to modify the script for instructional purposes to meet the needs of their individual classrooms.

Finally, the frame-of-reference model was purposefully designed to present the maximum amount of information needed for most teachers to follow the development. This is in contrast to the more typical approach in the preparation of mathematics and mathematics education materials, which generally attempts to present the development in a more "elegant" treatment (i.e., with a minimal amount of information). This approach of presenting the maximum amount of information became the cornerstone of the frame-of-reference model for an important reason.

Simply, most people who study mathematics or read mathematics-related materials are familiar with phrases in texts such as, "It is obvious that . . ." or "It follows therefore . . ." or "The conclusion is evident. . . ." Such phrases emphasize a major problem in preparing effective materials for school-based teachers of mathematics. Effectively, what happens in the preparation of materials about mathematics is that the author strives to present the information in as brief, crisp, and concise a development as possible. This is a version of the notion of "elegance" in mathematics. In the process, the author assumes that readers of the material have certain levels of background knowledge that will enable them to consider the material and follow the author's presentation with relative ease.

Unfortunately, far too often, the assumptions authors make about the reader's background in mathematics are wrong. They may be correct in the sense that persons with the background assumed by the writer should be able to follow the development. But they are clearly wrong in the sense that few readers will actually have these assumed characteristics. Therefore, what is obvious to the author in writing the materials frequently is not obvious to many readers, particularly when the readership has the wide range of abilities and background experiences found among classroom teachers.

Instead of making my own judgments about what readers would need to know in order to follow a development, it seemed reasonable to take the opposite approach--that is, to provide a comprehensive treatment of materials so that each individual reader could make judgments about what to read and what not to read. The idea is that by having material that was complete, the reader is free to read, skim, or skip selected portions of the material as appropriate. In other words, control over what will be read is given to the reader, not the writer.

Preliminary tests of the frame-of-reference model were quite successful. Many readers appreciated the in-depth treatment and found it relatively easy to decide what to read, what to skim, and what to skip. Admittedly, initial reactions of some readers of early drafts of the book were that the development seemed a bit tedious to read. At first, these readers found the presentation *too* comprehensive. But as they considered the material over time, these same readers often found that the in-depth treatment and the comprehensive nature of the material presented enabled them more easily to follow the development, understand the ideas presented, review the material quickly at a later time, and translate the ideas into actual teaching lessons for their own classes.

Thus was born the frame-of-reference model. The goal of this model is to provide written resource materials to the range of teachers who might benefit from seeing how manipulatives can be used effectively to teach mathematics content. Because of the in-depth way in which the materials are written and presented, the decision about what should or should not be read to understand the development is left in the hands of the reader, not the author of the materials.